NOW THIS IS A VERY TRUE STORY

NOW THIS IS A VERY TRUE STORY

THE AUTOBIOGRAPHY OF A COMEDY LEGEND

JIMMY JONES

WITH GARRY BUSHELL

FOREWORD BY NICKO MCBRAIN, IRON MAIDEN

JOHN BLAKE

Published by John Blake Publishing Ltd,
3 Bramber Court, 2 Bramber Road,
London W14 9PB, England

www.johnblakepublishing.co.uk

First published in hardback in 2010

ISBN: 9781843581963

British Library Cataloguing-in-Publication Data:

A catalogue record for this book is available from the British Library.

Design by www.envydesign.co.uk

Printed in the UK by CPI William Clowes Beccles NR34 7TL

1 3 5 7 9 10 8 6 4 2

Papers used by John Blake Publishing are natural, recyclable
products made from wood grown in sustainable forests. The
manufacturing processes conform to the environmental
regulations of the country of origin.

All pictures from the author's collection except where indicated.
Every attempt has been made to contact the relevant copyright-holders,
but some were unobtainable. We would be grateful if the appropriate
people could contact us.

To….

Dolly, Dave and family for all of their support and
love during many difficult times.

And,
To Marion,
because you are who you are.

ACKNOWLEDGEMENTS

My thanks go to Jack Sharpe, Neil Warnock and a whole host of agents and promoters too numerous to mention.

To all of the backroom staff at every venue where I have performed.

To Garry Bushell for helping to make this book happen.

To Garry Elwood for his advice and assistance.

To Mick Pugh and Paul Ross for giving freely of their time and Tania Bushell for transcribing the interviews.

And lastly to *you*, my public – for your undying support during my 50 years in show business.

THANK YOU.

CONTENTS

FOREWORD

NICKO MCBRAIN

I'D HEARD OF Jimmy Jones but I'd never seen him – his reputation went before him. So the first night I was due to work with him I was really nervous. I didn't know what to expect. We were in Gullivers, a Mayfair nightclub, back in the early 1970s and Jim had his own room in the basement which was called Kinnell's in honour of his catchphrase.

I sat at a table in the little balcony, stage right, and surveyed the audience. Keith Emerson, the legendary keyboard player was there, a couple of starlets, a minor Royal, and I wondered what I was letting myself in for. Then Jim started. He grabbed the audience by the throat and didn't let up. I was in hysterics from the off. Jimmy had a lot of one-liners back then and the pace was relentless. I was actually hurting from laughing at him. And when I got the call to go on stage I didn't know how I'd manage it. How would it be possible to play the drums when you were cracking up?

With most shows, the band might watch the star's act once

or twice and after that they'd tend to spend the rest of the shows at the bar. But Jimmy Jones was so funny I didn't miss a single performance. I saw every one of his shows and they were always a riot. I was a fan for life.

Unfortunately, Jim wasn't much of a fan of my drumming. As you'll see later in this book, he gave me the sack because my drumming was too loud. I put dusters on and everything but I was still too much for Jim and I was out – the rotten bastard!

He was up front about it, though, and he did apologise. It was impossible to stay mad at him, because he's such a wonderful man. You couldn't wish to meet a nicer gentleman. He's straight down the line, too. What you see is what you get with Jim. That's what endeared him to me. He never takes anything or anyone for granted. And he's funny off-stage as well. He doesn't crack jokes all the time; it's just that larger-than-life personality of his. He can't help but make you grin.

I was lucky enough to get to know Jim socially and spend time with his family. Once I went to Sunday dinner at his house in Essex with Phil Hilborne, the blues guitarist. We had a great time, a few beers, some stories. Jim's wife Marion cooked up a smashing roast. Jimmy's only job was to carry in the peas but somehow he managed to trip up and the peas went everywhere. Most blokes would have gone ballistic. Not Jim. He just looked back and said, 'Kinnell, who put that rug there?' Then we were all down on our hands and knees picking up the peas before Marion could see what had happened. They tasted great! A bit of grit and shit doesn't hurt anyone.

Ten years after Gullivers, I joined Iron Maiden. Sitting in the tour bus, I started telling a few Jimmy Jones gags and it turned out that the boys all loved him as well – we used to play his tapes on the road, as a lot of rock bands did. We would have Jimmy Jones nights on tour where we'd all sit around re-telling his greatest jokes. We invited him down to a few of our shows and parties. He's performed at charity bashes for us. We all love him to bits.

Some po-faced people take Jones the wrong way. I was angry on his behalf back in the '80s when certain councils banned him from performing at their venues. Yes, his act is brutal, but that's comedy. There was never any offence meant – I know that because I've known Jimmy Jones well for 37 years.

I'm proud and happy to say that as well as being a living legend he's a great person, and a true friend.

Nicko McBrain, September 2010

INTRODUCTION

GARRY BUSHELL

AS JIMMY JONES jumps off the stage and walks through the audience, the people closest to him squirm like live bait in a bucket. Those who have been before know what to expect and they brace themselves accordingly.

A bashful young blonde is the first to enjoy a personal encounter with the legendary Cockney comedian. 'Look at your hand shaking,' Jimmy says. He flashes the rest of us an evil grin and adds, in a voice heavy with suggestion, 'It seems a shame to waste it...'

He pauses and adds: 'I've got a little treat for you later on, and it won't melt in your hand.'

A busty brunette behind her tries hard to keep a straight face. 'Don't look so serious my dear,' Jones says with mock concern. Pause, beat. 'You might have yer dates wrong... Is that your 'usband? *Lucky bastard!*'

He goes on in a conspiratorial tone. 'I pulled a bird in 'ere last night,' he tells the couple. 'She said, "Give me 12 inches and hurt me." So I pushed it in six times and punched her in the ear-hole.'

They're laughing now, but Jones hasn't finished with her old man. 'Did she buy you that shirt, mate?' Jimmy asks. The bloke nods.

'She must 'kin' hate you!'

'What you doing wearing a shirt like that, you scatty bastard?' The crowd are in hysterics, Jones decides to soften the blow. 'No, it looks good…' he assures him, turning to the rest of us and saying in a loud stage whisper: 'I'd 'kin' burn it!'

He moves on to a smart blonde in a white halter neck. 'Where are you from, darling? Talk to Jim. Where? East Grinstead? Oh they're posh there, they get out of the bath to have a piss, don't they? Not like us, we piss in the flannel and wring it out. Look at you all in white, you bloody liar! Which one's your husband? Go on, which one? It's this one here, isn't it? Haven't you got little hands, I bet it don't half make his dick look big.'

Jones turns to the crowd. 'Well it's true! Well it's no good going out with a bird who has got big hands, she's got hold of your dick and you've got none left. You wanna see your helmet hanging over the end, don't you?'

Laughter, applause; heads nod in agreement. 'Have you got any kids, my darling? Yes? How many? Six! Strewth. Must be something in the air down there' – beat – 'possibly yer legs.'

I was a teenager in the early '70s when I first saw Jimmy Jones live in South London. I had never laughed so much in my life. Jones was already a legend in working class circles –

they even played his tapes on picket lines. But nothing had prepared me for the full onslaught of his live show. Gag after gag came flying at us. There were one-liners, 'true stories', bad taste jokes delivered in cod accents, and plenty of good-natured banter with the crowd – especially the women. The humour was as broad as the Thames is at Greenwich.

On paper now, and seen through today's narrow PC-tinted spectacles, some of Jim's material inevitably seems 'offensive'. But the atmosphere at his pilchard-packed gigs was warmer than the goods that changed hands in most of the backstreet London pubs and clubs he was performing in. Jimmy Jones managed something magical: he created his own comedy universe. He was also the first ever British comic to release adult stand-up on record and later on video.

The world of Jones was similar to the *Carry On* movies but much bluer. It was a world driven mostly by sex, where lengths were slipped and portions were enthusiastically delivered.

It was filth, but compared to today's humour, it was almost wholesome. Jones famously didn't swear at first, instead he had his own catchphrase: 'Kinnell!' which he claimed was short for 'blinking hell – and you can please yer 'kin' selves if you 'kin' believe me or you 'kin' don't.'

The 'C' word never crossed his lips; nor did the 'W' word. Masturbation was a 'five knuckle shuffle' while a woman's privates were her Jack and Danny.

'How are you up the back?' he'd shout to people sitting at the rear of the venue. *'Do you like it up the back?'*

Some of his jokes were delivered in a broad West Indian accent, which by the late 1980s led him to being condemned as 'racist' as well as 'sexist' by the usual suspects. Yet I've known Jimmy well for more than 25 years, I've even holidayed with him, and I know that there's not a gram of bigotry in him. That's because Jim wouldn't have anything to do with the metric system; he only thinks in imperial measures...

Seriously, there's not an ounce of racism in him. His former manager Neil Warnock, who was married to the black English pop star Linda Lewis, recalls the time they stopped for a beer in the Red Lion in Leytonstone. 'There were a whole bunch of black Cockney guys playing snooker in there and as soon as they saw Jimmy they started doing *his* West Indian accent back at him. They loved him. Jim was never prejudiced. As he said, he told jokes about everybody. The only people who didn't get it were the middle class left-wing media.'

Jimmy's act has to be judged in its setting which was the popular culture of the 1970s, a time when TV shows like *It Ain't Half Hot Mum* and *Love Thy Neighbour* were both a ratings smash, Bernard Manning was a mainstream star and *Till Death Us Do Part* was still going strong.

Jones was the first blue comic to break big. His act made him a working class hero to hundreds of thousands of blue collar Londoners. He became an underground legend, as well as a small black market industry churning out his act on vinyl, audio cassettes, Betamax and VHS years ahead of any other comic. The most unexpected people were drawn to his shows. Jimmy attracted rock stars, such as The Rolling Stones, The

Nice, the Small Faces, Iron Maiden, Status Quo and the Cockney Rejects. The Beatles played his tapes on their tour bus. His fans ranged from fellow comedians like Dudley Moore to soap stars such as Martine McCutcheon, Peter Dean and Dean Gaffney, via Hollywood legends like Tom Selleck.

When the late great Benny Hill went to see Jim at a nightclub once, he told him: 'If you see my hand moving under the table I'm only making notes.'

Jones has told jokes to Michael Jackson; he's entertained the Kray Twins – and their South London rivals the Richardson brothers – and has been booked for private shows by the editor of the country's biggest-selling daily newspaper. Most surprisingly of all, Jimmy has performed for most of the senior members of the Royal Family, including Prince Philip, Prince Charles and Princess Margaret. His natural audience may have been dockers and dustmen, but Jones went down well with dukes and duchesses too.

Not bad going for a kid from a dirt poor East London background who thought he'd grow up to be a priest.

To this day religion figures strongly in his humour, though Lord alone knows what the good sisters of St Ethelburga's Catholic School would make of his bishop and nun gag, punch-line: 'He told me it was Gabriel's horn and I've been blowing it for five years.'

In the late 1980s Jimmy Jones would sell out the Circus Tavern in Purfleet, Essex, for 15 weeks of the year – that's six, sometimes seven nights a week, playing to 1100 people a night. At the time he was a bigger draw than his 'apprentice'

Jim Davidson, who was a TV regular – something Jimmy Jones would never be. Jimmy was a victim of his own notoriety. Telly bosses hated him to an irrational degree. Only Arthur Daley's missus has made fewer small screen appearances.

Although one senior ITV executive did once offer Jim prime time exposure in return for sex with the lovely lady who is now his wife. But Jimmy Jones's outrageous comedy had made him a millionaire by the time he was 50. He was the first English comic to receive a gold disc for comedy album sales. He has generated DVD, video, album and audio cassette sales worth more than £10m.

'The bastards won't let me on TV,' he shrugs. 'I dunno why. I personally think that I could brighten up *In The Night Garden*. I'd give that Upsy Daisy one upsy back...'

CHAPTER ONE

IN THE 'KIN' BEGINNING – ROAMIN' CATHOLIC

I have got a story for you tonight that is true. A fella got on a bus, single decker bus; there's only one seat right down the front by the driver, and sitting next to the window is this nun. So he went and sat next to this nun, and as he looks at this nun, he's done a double take.

He says, 'Excuse me sister, I don't mean to stare at you but you're beautiful and you're a 'kin' nun and all.

'Would you think of leaving the order to marry me?'

She said, 'I'm ever so sorry my son, but I'm married to God.'

He said 'Sister, I don't mean to be a 'kin' nuisance but I think you meet the one you're going to marry like that and you're 'kin' her.

'Would you not even think about it?'

She said, 'I'm sorry, that's very, very flattering but I'm married to God. Excuse me.' And with that she got up and got off the bus.

So the bus driver says, 'I couldn't help but overhear you,

1

mush, you've got a 'kin' lovely line of patter. You've made her excited, she's got fruity, she's had to get off the 'kin' bus.

'Do you know the church in the meadow?'

He said, 'Yes, very well.'

The driver said, 'Well if it's any help to you I reckon you could pull her. She goes down there every morning at six o'clock for morning prayers; you get yourself down there and you can 'kin' chat her up.'

The fella said, 'I'll give that a try.'

So he got himself a big white wig, a 'kin' beard, Jesus sandals. Quarter to six he's standing behind a 'kin' tree, waiting. It's still dark. He sees this nun walking across the meadow so he jumps out from behind this tree.

She says, 'Jesus!'

He said, 'That's right my child. And you are married to me,' he said, 'and I have come down to earth to consummate the marriage.'

'Oh,' she said, 'you've picked the 'kin' wrong week.'

So Jesus says, 'That's a 'kin' nuisance, I've got the horn now.'

She said, 'Well I don't mind taking a bit up the back.'

'Oh,' he said, 'all right', so her turned her round, lent her up against a tree and wallop, he's given her one up the back. But when he was finished he was overcome with remorse. He thinks to himself, I'm a dirty bastard I've 'kin' rumped a nun.

So he turns to her, takes off the wig and says: 'I'm sorry, sister. I've got a confession to make. I'm not Jesus, I'm the bloke off the bus.'

The nun says to him: 'Well I've got a confession to make and all, I'm not the nun. I'm the bus driver...'

It's true! I'm doing that on *Stars On Sunday* 'cos it's religious...

I WAS BORN at a very early age on 9 February 1938. My mother was in labour so long the midwife had to shave her twice. I can't believe I spent two days getting out of there and the next 72 years trying to get back in. It's the only hobby I've ever had, and it's cost me a fortune. Read on...

I was the sixth child of a family of seven. I had four elder sisters – Jean, Anne, Margaret and Mary; but Mary is the only one of the girls still alive. My brother Patrick was already in the RAF when I was born and Dad was never home, so I was raised in a house full of girls. I grew up being bossed around by women... Nothing changes.

My brother Pat's still going strong. He's 14 years older than I am, so he decided to call me The General Nuisance, hence my family nickname is The General. I had two brothers born after me; one was named Anthony, but unfortunately he died at birth, and my younger brother, Michael, is still with us.

The worse thing about growing up poor in a big family full of sisters was the hand-me-downs were hell. Imagine turning up for PE in the wrong colour knickers. I wore a dress until I was 11.

I had a happy childhood, though, and I was spoilt rotten by the older girls. It was like having four mums – most of the time. The other thing to remember though is that when a load of women live together their cycles tend to get in tandem with each other, so for one week every month I felt like getting on me bike and fucking off myself. Except I didn't have a bike, we couldn't afford one, and you can't get far with a hoop and a stick.

We were a very religious family. Mother, Jean, was Irish and a devoted Catholic. Albert, my father, was raised a Protestant but he converted. They met in service, mother was a chambermaid and father was a waiter in a private house in Southampton. He was originally from Godalming, in Surrey, mother was from Dublin.

I was born in Southampton – so I was destined to be a saint. What went wrong?

When I was three months old, the church moved our family to Rainham in Essex, just on the borders of the East End. I didn't see much of my father after that because he became a merchant seaman. He sailed round the world eight times. By complete coincidence mother had eight children. He only came home to dip his wick! Lecherous old bastard!

I nicknamed him Percy because he kept his money in a little purse... But he was a proper Percy Filth. Like father like son, says my wife Marion. Percy applies to my life too, as I have a lot in common with that film, *Percy's Progress*. You might not believe me but it's 12 inches, and I don't use it as a rule.

It was the war years and at the age of seven, I became an altar boy at La Salette church in Rainham. Luckily none of the priests ever tried to alter me. La Salette was a US Catholic church with connections to Lourdes. I only signed up because I like cricket. Well, they did have a bat in the vestry...

Because I lived the nearest to the church and Mum was such a staunch Catholic I always got the 7.30 mass.

We had several American priests there, and I got on exceptionally well with one of them in particular by the name of Father Hayes.

Being a Catholic, I was educated by nuns. I went to Roman Catholic schools, St Peter's School in Dagenham and the St Ethelburga's Catholic School in Barking. I was full of mischief even at primary school. I wasn't a really bad kid, but I was cheeky. I got up to things and tried it on.

I was beaten by one nun for smoking when I was seven. In those days the nuns wore black habits with a big long leather belt and I can still remember the pain. Sister Stephanie caught me with a roll-up smoking in the toilets and she gave me a good hiding with that leather belt. She slapped me across the back of my legs with her strap and that did me a favour because from that day on I've never smoked again.

It annoys me when all these do-gooders say you mustn't give kids a good hiding. That's why they don't know how to behave anymore. I'd bring back conscription. Give 'em all 18 months in the Kate – the Kate Karney, the army.

The other great hiding I got at school was by the music teacher, Sister Dominique now isn't it marvellous how you can remember these names all these years later? She gave me a hiding with her belt that Max Mosley would have paid good money for. My crime this time was not paying attention in music classes and as a consequence I went on to become a singer – so it works!

Another favourite punishment was to make us take off our shoes and socks and stand bare-foot on the radiator. So naturally, I behaved myself in winter, but when it came to the summer I was a right little bastard.

At that time I really thought I was going to be a priest. As well as being an altar boy, I was singing in the choir, and as certain orders of priests travelled the world, I was convinced that this was the thing to be. But when I found out I couldn't be Pope I said 'Fuck 'em.'

Seriously, when I was nine, Sister Dominique said to me, 'I think God has given you a natural talent to entertain. God gave you your voice, use it.' She taught me about how to breathe when you sing, saying, 'If you learn to breathe correctly you will sing correctly'.

That same year, still aged nine, I was singing in a talent competition at Rainham Working Men's Club and a fella came up to me and said, 'I want you to join my band.' He went and saw my Mum and sorted it out. Luckily for me it wasn't Jonathan King. His name was Mr Gregory – I always called him that. The Gregory Family had a band called The Hilly-Billy Pennies, which makes them sound like they should have all had red necks, no teeth and discarded fridges on the lawn outside of their trailers, but they were actually a very good country and western band who played extensively in the local area. And when I say local, I mean Rainham Social Club, Rainham Working Men's Club, and the Silver Hall Social Club in New Road... Rainham. You could do a tour and still be home by nine o'clock.

Top of the shop in those days for us was the Dagenham Working Men's Club, which was considered the number one venue on our little circuit. We used to do odd nights there. There was never any wages or anything else like that but they were good days.

Then at the age of ten I was poached by another fella for his band, the Rainham Nitwits. They were a bazooka band – they used brass wind instruments which harmonised with my voice. His name was Charlie Cutbush and his wife had some smashing bazookas of her own.

Charlie was *the* florist of Rainham. He'd been a police special during the war, and I came to see him as a father figure. I hadn't seen my real father for a long, long time because he was still away at sea for most of the year. He was the head waiter on the *Queen Mary* by this time and with my brother Pat off with the air force, I had no strong male influence in my life up until then and I'd grown up totally ignorant about sex. Things like that were never ever talked about at home. I thought my knob was just for pissing out of and that wanking was a town in China; provided no one was Peking.

All of that changed when I was 12 years old, though. I was on a variety bill at the Rainham Working Men's Club and this 17-year-old dancer called Margaret White caught me and my friend Peter Gregory hiding under the billiard table watching her and the other dancers getting changed. She was quite a good-looking girl, and very fit. She marched me out the back of the club, took me into a field and led me out of my state of darkness. She said, 'I'm going to do to you what my boyfriend does to me.' And she did and all! Talk about sinking the pink. That was all the sex education I ever had, or ever needed.

I lost my cherry 500 yards from the Cherry Tree pub.

Not long after that, Charlie Cutbush took me under his wing and he asked my mother could he become my legal guardian. She agreed because she thought it was important for me to learn a trade. The plan was for me to become a florist, and so I stayed at Charlie's house in Lambs Lane and I was getting up at 4am with him and going up to Covent Garden market which was the place to go for fruit, flowers and veg. What an introduction to the world of men that was. The market was a riot of noise and smells and slang. Charlie would choose the flowers and back we'd come home and we'd make moss weaves and so on. I used to make my fingers bleed, stubbling – a florist's term – bits of wire into the flowers.

Charlie also had land where he used to grow his own flowers and at certain times of the year he grew tomatoes inside this massive greenhouse. My job was to pick them and sell them for him. I'd flog them at Rainham Working Men's Club and around the CIU (working men's clubs) union circuit during the week; and at the weekends I'd be singing. The band never had a set fee, but what they used to do in those days, when I got up and sang, they'd have a whip round for me and sometimes I got as much as 30 bob (£1.50p) which was good money for me. I used to give my mum a pound of it and I'd keep 10 bob for meself. Her face would light up with pride.

Growing up we had the one thing money can't buy: poverty. As a family we were dirt poor. If I hadn't been a boy I wouldn't have had anything to play with. It didn't help that my father had a terrible gambling problem. What little he did make was more likely to go on William Hill's than the family bills.

We didn't have money but then nobody down our way did. Everyone in Rainham was hard-up. We were so poor, our rainbows were in black and white. And you wouldn't find a pot of gold at the end of them, more like a rusty bike. But when you think about it, we didn't really need money. We didn't have X-Boxes and iPods and computer games like today's kids have come to take for granted. All I used to spend on myself was six old pennies (two and a half pence) for Saturday morning pictures. I'd go to the Princess Cinema Dagenham every Saturday and that tanner would get me in and buy me a packet of Larkin's Roasted Peanuts. Seeing Roy Rogers and The Three Stooges was the only luxury in my life.

In some ways I think we were better off like that. We learnt to appreciate the simple things in life. One of my grand-kids was showing me a computer game the other day and he said, 'Look at this grandad, it's so life-like I could be playing outside.' Well, why not play outside then? It'd be a lot healthier tearing about in the fresh air than sitting indoors playing a computer game.

At 11, I moved on to big school – at St Ethelburga's in Barking – and the poverty came with me. Because we never used to have any money, I got free school dinners. There was no free bus passes back then either, so I had to walk to school.

We didn't have an inside bog. But my mate's family had it worse. They didn't have an outside bog either. If you were there and you needed a Jimmy, they'd tell you to use the third tree on the left.

That was a joke, obviously. They couldn't afford trees.

I had no decent clobber back then; I didn't even have a proper pair of shoes or a pair of boots to play football in. Football back then was something else. It wasn't just jumpers for goal posts. Picture this: 38-a-side with a rolled-up newspaper for a ball and wellies for football boots... and they wondered how we won the World Cup in 1966. Give us kids a proper ball and a pair of boots and watch us go!

Alf Ramsey, Terry Venables, Bobby Moore, Martin Peters and Jimmy Greaves were all born within five miles of me. I rest my case.

You never realise the blessing of being born poor until you get over it.

Charlie Cutbush was very good with me; he had a whistle made for me by a tailor off of Petticoat Lane, and a handmade shirt and took a bit out of my wages every week to pay for it. Charlie saw me all right.

*   *   *   *

I'm afraid I can't tell you much about my secondary school – I was never there! I only used to go to music lessons. I'm not proud of that. I didn't learn the things I should. Reading is still a problem. Now they would have said that I was dyslexic. Actually I was dyslexic and ambidextrous – I couldn't write with either hand.

In reality I was just a cheeky bastard who hopped the wag.

But not being able to read properly has held me back. I missed out on two big film roles in the 1980s because of it, two London crime films. They wanted me for the parts but I couldn't read the scripts. A shame, I think I'd have made a very good Violet Kray. But I've got no one to blame but myself.

I was 12 when I saw my father again. I have a vivid memory of him coming home from the *Queen Mary* and him saying to my mum, 'We're going out tonight and we're taking Albert with us.' He'd got us tickets to see a show and it was a night I'll never forget it as long as I live. We went to the East Ham Palace Theatre which meant getting a bus ride to Dagenham East and then the train straight to East Ham; and as you got out at East Ham, there was East Ham Palace. I was thrilled but when we got there they wouldn't let me in, they said, 'No, he's too young.' My dad said, 'But the gentleman who is the top of the bill gave me the tickets'. So they told him to go round and see him and we went back stage.

Top of the bill that night was a front of cloth comedian – a common expression for someone who might do his patter with the curtains down behind him while stagehands rearranged the set for the next turn. This one was the greatest who ever lived – Max Miller. Max greeted my father warmly and said: 'Albert, do you want him to see me?' and he said, 'Yes I do, I don't see anything wrong with you Max.' Max said, 'In that case then, he can come backstage with me, you can go outside and enjoy the show and come back and see me afterwards.'

And so I watched Max Miller perform from the wings and

witnessed the charisma of this man. Some of the jokes went over my head, but some of them I remember to this day and some I even did in my act, like the deaf and dumb man who got married and his wife made him wear boxing gloves in bed to stop him talking in his sleep... or the fella who was promised two acres and a cow by his future father-in-law for marrying his daughter and who concludes ruefully, 'I'm still waiting for the two acres.'

In those days, the most the turns used to do was about a 20-minute act, but Max was on stage for the whole of the second half. It was just pure magic watching him work the crowd; he got them on his side and blamed them for laughing at the more suggestive gags, saying, 'You wicked lot. You're the type of people who give me a bad name.' He left his limericks open-ended: 'When roses are red/They're ready for plucking/When a girl is 16/She's ready for... 'ere! 'ere!'

He was flamboyant, outrageous and sensational. He looked terrific too in his dazzling silk suit, plus-fours, kipper tie, white shoes and that immaculate white trilby hat. He'd say, 'I know exactly what you're thinking, you're thinking, why is he dressed like that? I'll tell you why I'm dressed like this, I'm a commercial salesman and I'm ready for bed!'

After the show, Max sat and chatted to me in his dressing room and he told me he'd run away from home at 14 to join the circus. My father came back round to collect me, Max poured him a drink and he thanked my father very much for looking after him while he was on the ship, 'cos Max had done a cruise. And then – I'll always remember it – he turned and said, 'Do you know what, Albert? The establishment hate me, but they have to work me because I put bums on seats.' And it was true, wherever he went there was always a 'House Full' sign outside, and it was an encounter that I will always, always remember and cherish.

Father went back to sea shortly afterwards, and my other dad Charlie Cutbush continued to be a huge influence. Between the ages of 12 and 16 I went out singing. I'd get up early to go to Covent Garden, kip in the afternoon and then go out and sing in the evening. Often this would be at Broadstreet Working Men's Club in Dagenham where in those days the compère, believe it or not, was the great London entertainer Max Bygraves. He used to have a wonderful Cockney song called 'Chip-Chopper Charlie' about a fish shop boss who fell into the batter and got served up instead of the fish.

I would also sing at Millhouse Social Club, also in Dagenham, and there were some villains in there I can assure you, some very big villains. The joke at the time was that if they liked you at the Millhouse they let you live. The club was bang opposite the big Ford plant in the days when Ford was in full swing. Do you know how many people worked there at this time? About half of them.

I started to go further afield, performing at places like the Civic Theatre in Poplar, and wherever there was a talent competition going on I would enter it.

I was very lucky in those days and won my share of contests; I used to sing and whistle. I did bird impressions; no, not like

Lily Savage, proper birds. And I became known as 'Albert Simmonds the Whistling Wonder'. Well that's what someone in the audience called me, and it sounded like wonder.

That same year I won my first talent show under that billing. That was called Carroll Levis Discoveries, which was the *X Factor* of its day, only it was on the radio and you didn't have to have a family member at death's door before you could do it...

I went on tour with Carroll Levis at the age of 12. We played the Moss Empires music halls and I would do two songs a show. I used to sing 'If I Were A Blackbird' and whistle 'In The Monastery Garden'. Not a safe thing to do for a young boy these days if the papers can be believed.

Charlie Cutbush was with me at the time and he was asked if I'd like to do a radio show advertising Star Razor Blades. This was on Radio Luxemburg, Star Razor Blades were the show's sponsors, and I sang and whistled there. And I sang and whistled 'The Whiffenpoof Song', a Bing Crosby hit; people knew it then as 'Three Little Lambs': 'We're poor little lambs who have lost our way, baa, baa, baa...'

The show went out on the Friday night, and the next night when we got to the Finsbury Park Empire, Carroll Levis was not in the best of moods. He told me he'd heard me on the radio the day before and that he thought I was good, but then he turned and said 'Why?' I explained that Mr Cutbush was offered the opportunity for me to do the radio show and advised me to do it. Carroll Levis explained that the Luxemburg show's host, Hughie Green, was his opposition. 'I hate the man,' he said, with real conviction. 'And so after tonight you no longer will be on my show.' And that was how I lost the Carroll Levis Discoveries tour. That I suppose was the consequence of not having a manager who knew about the entertainment business. Charlie was doing his best but he was a florist. He didn't have any idea about showbiz rivalries and the etiquette of it all and, as a young boy of 12, neither did I.

Years later I also went in for *Opportunity Knocks* and won that, too.

That was while I was working at the Royal Standard in Walthamstow. I was 23 and I'd become a full time professional by this time, and I'd started to have some trouble with my throat because I was working too much. I was advised that drinking port and brandy would clear my throat for me but all it really meant was that I was getting as pissed as a rat every night. In the end, I went to my doctor and he told me I needed to have my tonsils out. So I had the op and was told to rest my voice, and couldn't work for three whole weeks. Luckily the publican, Lou Wheatley, was very kind to me because by then I had five children and she kept me afloat. In the middle of this recuperation period I had a letter from Hughie Green to appear on *Op Knocks*. In those days I was still singing and whistling, and Hughie wanted me to perform 'Edelweiss' from the Rodgers & Hammerstein musical *The Sound of Music*, a big hit for Vince Hill at the time.

Lou Wheatley took me into London and bought me a beautiful blazer and matching pair of trousers for the show. She did me up from my shoes to my head, I really looked the business, and we went up on the train together to Didsbury in Manchester, but when we got there the producer said, 'No, we don't like the suit it looks horrible.' I said 'What do you mean it's horrible? This is a lovely whistle.'

But the producer was most insistent that the suit didn't go with the song. And so he got wardrobe to provide me with a rotten old carpenter's woolly and I had to stand on a bridge that they'd built with all these white flowers dotted around.

When we got back to the Royal Standard that night, the place went mad. People loved seeing one of their own on TV and they were wishing me luck for the next week, but I already knew I wouldn't win again because Hughie had told me there was a kid coming on from Wales who played the violin: Hughie said the Welsh would write letters backing him by the lorry-load.

The deal back then that the public didn't know about was that if you won the show two weeks in a row you had to sign up to Hughie Green's management company and give him 25 per cent of your earnings. I let it be known that I wouldn't be up for that and so the second week I lost to that little kid from Wales who played the violin. He wasn't the only one on the fiddle.

CHAPTER TWO

WELCOME TO THE HOUSE OF FUN

I WAS STILL a teenager when I found out firsthand about the fringe benefits of a life in showbusiness. At the age of 16, like most kids at the time, I bought myself a motorbike. It was the next door neighbour's 125 Excelsior, and I bought it off him for £25 which I raised by working for good old Charlie Cutbush.

I'd passed my driving test by then. I still used to see Charlie but not as much as before, because I'd got myself a job on a building site as a plasterer's labourer. I used to hang out at the Four Oaks, a bikers' cafe on the A13. It was owned by a fella called Tommy Asquith, who used to have his own puppet show. He'd heard me singing one night in the Silver Lion Social Club which was at the back of the café and he invited me to do a show with him at the Guisborough Social Club in North Yorkshire – four nights, Thursday to Sunday, for eight quid. He said you can follow me up, do the show and I'll pay for your digs as well, which sounded to me like a result.

When we got up there on the Thursday he introduced me to the club secretary whose house I was staying at, and told me he'd put me on not before the interval, but the act before that. I couldn't figure out why he'd done it until that night. The act who followed me was a magician, I'll never forget it. Right in the middle of his major trick with all the doves, the club chairman banged on the table and said, 'T'pies have arrived,' in an accent that could have been scrapped off the walls of 'kin' Kinsley colliery. He was so Northern he made Colin Compton sound posh. Immediately the audience got up and left him right in the middle of the bloody trick; they didn't give him a chance, they all wanted a pie. Even the doves were queuing up. And Tommy said, 'Now you know why I put you in second on the bill in the first half.' This kind of thing was par for the course in the Northern clubs. Peter Kay's *Phoenix Nights* could have been a documentary.

Tommy was the big act, and he used to close the show. That night, the club secretary took me home, gave me a bit of supper and introduced me to his daughter Maureen who was a stunning young girl who looked about my age. She had blonde hair, blue eyes and a lovely pair of bristols; she had a cute smile too and she was very flirty.

In the middle of the night this Maureen came and crept in bed with me and what followed was as wonderful as it was inevitable. When we finished, she kissed me on the cheek, got up and went back in her own bed.

This happened on the Thursday night, the Friday night and the Saturday night. I shafted her all over the weekend. I was leaving on the Monday morning, so on the Sunday night her father gave me a pull and said, 'Don't keep Maureen up too late tonight, she's got to get up for school in the morning.' That frightened the bleedin' life out of me, I can tell you. We got in the bed and I said to her, well how old are you? She said, 'I'm 14.'

For crying out loud! I knew the law at that time and I thought, I could be nicked here! It frightened me because I'd given her enough rod to put a hand-rail round Harrogate.

But I still gave her one before I fucked off.

The following morning I was up with the cock – again, on the motorbike and off like a bloody rocket. I didn't even say goodbye to her. My bike was older than Maureen was. Granted she had better acceleration and a quieter exhaust, but at least the motorbike was legal to ride.

Looking back now, I consider those three days as a bit of a Triumph.

*   *   *   *

I'd left school at 15 with no qualifications. I could add up, nobody would ever have me over for a quid, but even now my writing looks like a spider has crawled over the paper. I was a grafter, though, and the bike made me properly independent. I could drive myself to work and to shows. I didn't have to rely on anyone else any more, which was just how I liked it.

By the age of 17, people started to take notice of me. I was working the British Legion club down the Walworth Road in south London. It was an odd place; the entertainment secretary always used to warn you not to stay on stage for an extra song after your allotted time. This was for the very good reason that, if you did, you'd be wasting your time as the train went by every half hour and rocked the building for so long no one would have heard you. All you could hear was the bloody train. Of course it wouldn't apply now because these days the trains are always delayed.

This particular night, Larry Parnes the famous impresario was in and he came backstage after I'd sung and asked me if I could raise £250. I said, 'Are you joking, it was hard enough raising £25 for me bike.' He said 'That's a pity because if you could raise £250 I could get you a record contract.' We used to call him 'Parnes, Shillings and Pence' cos Larry was very reluctant to part with a pound note.

Well I didn't have a snowman's chance in the Sahara of raising that kind of dough. I was only getting paid £1.50 for a show. There was more chance of me giving Princess Margaret one. But there was another guy on the bill with me by the name of Tommy Hicks from Bermondsey, and his mother and father had a greengrocer's at the time, and they raised the money for Tommy to take Larry up on his offer. And, of course, Tommy Hicks became Tommy Steele, who had his first hit a year later in 1956 with 'Rock With The Caveman', and his first Number One two months after that with 'Singin' The Blues'.

Just think, if I could have raised half a monkey that might have been me singing 'Half A Sixpence' on Broadway as opposed to singing for two and sixpence in the Broadway, Dagenham...

When I wasn't out working as a singer, I would still enter whatever talent shows were going and work for free. There were a few of us who used to go in for all of these contests at the time. It was generally the same little crew, you may have heard of them. There was Queenie Watts who became a famous actress, Tommy Bruce, who sounded a lot like Louis Armstrong and had a Top Three hit in 1960, the singer Kim Cordell from Clacton who did a bit of telly in the '60s, and a fella from Shoreditch by the name of Terry Parsons who changed his name and became an international showbusiness legend as Matt Monro.

Back then he was a bus driver; he worked out of Plaistow bus garage. He certainly rang the bell later on with massive international hits such as 'Born Free', 'Walk Away' and 'Softly As I Leave You'.

The best of these pub talent contests was at the Rising Sun in Bethnal Green on a Tuesday night. I'd win one week, Queenie would win the second, then Matt, then Tommy... and we'd all come back for the big final. It was very competitive and the standards were sky high – far higher than they are on TV talent shows today. So there started to be a bit of a buzz about the place. I was in the pub one night when the legendary Judy Garland came in to watch the turns. Eventually the Rising Sun talent nights inspired the ATV television series *Stars and Garters*, which tried to recreate the feel of a variety show in your local pub. It made stars of Kathy Kirby, Vince Hill and my old mate Tommy Bruce. The compère on the TV show was Ray Martine – not Welsh George who did it in the pub – but they did use the pub band, the Don Harvey Trio, who were to figure in my life a fair bit. There was Don Harvey on organ, Eric Cornish on drums and Jim Watkins on bass.

On TV, the audience consisted of extras mixed with real regulars from the Rising Sun. Only non-alcoholic drinks were served but they did hand out free cigarettes. Ray Martine was a good comic from the Deuragon Arms in Hackney, but his routine was so blue that ATV had to bring in Barry Cryer, Dick Vosburgh and Marty Feldman to write clean gags for him.

Back in the real world, the Rising Sun nights were such a runaway success that other pubs followed suit. A guy called Daniel Parsons started to run talent nights on the Isle of Dogs, with Martine as compère. He also put on a show called *A Night At The Comedy* in the West End with top turns such as Kenny Lynch and Vince Hill and a young up-and-coming Scouse comedian called Jimmy Tarbuck. Then he would have two acts competing in the new talent part of the show. One particular night, it was me versus Queenie Watts, and when Ray asked the audience who'd won, this one fella was most insistent. He said that Albert Simmonds was sensational and that he wanted to meet me after the show and give me his professional advice. I was thrilled and intrigued. It turned out he was a showbiz journalist called Godfrey Wynn from the *Sunday Express* – he was said to have been the highest paid columnist in Fleet Street, where his nickname was Winifred God. But Daniel and Ray pulled me over and said, 'Be careful of this bloke because he's not quite kosher'. I was 17 and didn't know what they were getting at, so they spelt it: the guy was gay, and quite predatory. He'd give me some column inches in the newspapers all right but he would also want to slip a column up the back – where *The Sun* don't shine.

Just as they'd predicted, I was propositioned straight afterwards. Godfrey came and spoke to me and his first words were, 'I could put you on top of the tree.'

And me, being a cocky little bastard, said, 'That's very kind of you but I'm not a fairy.' So there was my leg-up out the window, along with his leg-over.

Ray was gay himself, he just didn't like men with a thing for underage kids.

A Night At The Comedy was an absolutely fabulous show. Ray Martine had a sidekick in Kim Cordell, and there was another regular on the bill called Mrs Shufflewick who was a drag act and very, very funny indeed; Shufflewick was a legend in variety theatre circles. She was played by Rex Jameson, and the character was a drunken old Cockney charlady whose stories got dirtier the more she drank her port and lemon. We knew her as Shuff.

Jimmy Tarbuck closed the first half, and top of the bill was the brilliant Northern comedian Jimmy James who we all called Stumpy Marsh because he had a bad leg; Roy Castle was his stooge. Queenie Watts opened the second half with a song and then it was all down to Jimmy James. Tarbuck and I would sit and watch him six nights a week. We never missed a show. He was wonderful, a real comedian's comedian. We would just turn to each other and say, 'Look at his timing!' It was stunning, absolutely impeccable. He did a drunk sketch, an elephant in a box set, and his act was word perfect. It's an over-used phrase, but Jimmy James really was a comedy icon.

Ironically, off-stage James was a teetotaller, he wouldn't touch a drop, but no one played a better drunk. I can still see him now, lurching across the stage while 'Three O'Clock In The Morning' played in the background, his top hat askew, shirt out at the front, a wilting fag in his hand... wonderful. Jimmy's big problem was gambling. He loved a flutter and was declared bankrupt three or four times, but he was a very generous man. He got Bernard Manning his first agent, but then no one's perfect.

The show ran for about two months, maybe more, before the Lord Chancellor closed it. Because in the West End in those days, if you did anything even slightly naughty, if there was any bad language or risqué suggestions, then bang, the show would be closed. I remember the intense disappointment when I got there one Saturday night and the old boy on the stage door told me: 'Not tonight, Albert.'

'Why's that?'

'The Lord Chancellor was in at lunchtime, Mrs Shufflewick went over the top and they've closed the show.'

And that was it, Shuff had gone blue in the matinee and we all lost out. Some people in the cast said that was just an excuse and speculated that the real reason for closure was that Daniel Parsons had run out of money. I don't know if that was true, because we always played to packed houses, and besides, it didn't make any difference to me because I didn't really get paid anyway. But *A Night At The Comedy* ended for good that day. It would be a night with no comedy from now on.

I was never close to Jimmy Tarbuck but we were always friendly, and even now if I go into a theatre where he has appeared the night before he'll leave me a little note, along the lines of, 'Follow me around like this Jonesy and you'll soon be a star'.

As for Mrs Shufflewick, the problem was Rex was a pisshead. When Shuff was on at the Hackney Empire the production manager locked her in the dressing room to keep her off the pop but she was still getting legless and no one could work out how. Shuff was actually bribing a stage hand to buy half a bottle of whisky and stand outside the dressing room door while she drunk through the keyhole with a couple of joined-up straws. Her act got bluer the more she had to drink, so it was easy to see how she could have gone OTT at the matinee. I loved the act, it was all filth. She'd say things like: 'Do you like this fur, girls? It cost £200. I didn't pay for it meself; I met 200 fellas with a pound each... This is very rare, this fur. This is known in the trade as "untouched pussy" – which as you know is unobtainable in the West End of London at the moment. And I don't think there's much knocking around here tonight.'

She had a story about a shoemaker who made a pair of boots for Queen Victoria and stuck a sign in the window that read 'Cobblers To The Queen'. The Palace made him take it down, so he replaced it with another one: 'Bollocks To The King.'

*　　*　　*　　*

I was 18 when I met my first wife in the most romantic of locations, the Four Oaks café. All the herberts and ton-up boys used to get in there, the air was full of exotic aromas: frying bacon, the smell of coffee and petrol fumes. Gracie Lock was a good-looking girl. She caught my eye and we hit it off immediately. I laughed her into bed and the next thing I knew Gracie was pregnant. It was my fault, I should have taken precautions; I should have given her a false name.

Being a boy of 18 years of age I wasn't ready to settle down but my girlfriend was expecting and in those days it meant you got married. You were brought up to do the right thing. So I did. We tied the knot on 5 January 1957. And three months later, on St George's Day, 23 April, she gave birth to my lovely son Paul.

Not an ideal start to married life, but I'm immensely proud of my family: four boys and two girls, who have given me 17 grandchildren aged between ten and 31, and nine great grandchildren – ten by the time this book is published.

I couldn't keep a wife and my son afloat on the money I was making from my act, which was still singing, whistling and bird impressions, so I was working in the building trade as a plasterer until the guy I was working for very inconveniently went and died on me.

I got myself another job as a tiler's labourer which entailed exactly the same kind of thing – knocking off muck and hard work. I learnt to lay tiles, just as I'd learnt to become a plasterer, by picking the job up as I went along and helping out whenever I could.

WELCOME TO THE HOUSE OF FUN

At the time, Grace and I were living separately, her with her mum and me with mine, and then she went to live with a friend over in Dagenham. But I must have been making plenty of journeys over to see her because pretty soon she became pregnant again, this time with Helen.

To sort out our living arrangements, I finally met a lady councillor, turned on the charm and persuaded her that the council should give us a house. It was a right dump because the people living in it before had let it go to rack and ruin, but the council said we could have it providing I agreed to clear it up. I jumped at the chance. And that our first home together, 34 Sunnings Lane, Upminster.

To show what a family man I was, I traded my motorbike in for one with a side car. We had some fun and games on that. One night in particular we'd been visiting our parents in Rainham and were driving home, with my son on the back of the bike with me and my wife in the side car with the baby. It was near Christmas and this Old Bill stopped us on a country lane and demanded to know if I had any chickens in the side car. I said, 'You're having a laugh aren't you mate?'

Apparently a crowd of herberts had raided a local poultry farm and half-inched all the chickens. And this cop only made Grace and the baby get out of the side car so he could search it for chickens. The dozy bastard. We had plenty of stuffing back then, but no stolen chickens.

It was just as well I never volunteered to show him my prize cock.

JIMMY JONES

A chicken walks up to a duck at the side of road. He says, 'Whatever you do don't cross, mate, you'll never hear the 'kin' end of it.'

CHAPTER THREE

THE BOYS ON THE DOCKS

A bloke visiting Dagenham docks sees a docker on the floor writhing in agony.

'What's wrong with him?' he asks.

His union rep says, 'He needs a shit.'

'OK,' says the stranger. 'Why doesn't he just go the toilet?'

'What?' says the union rep. 'On his 'kin' dinner break?'

MY FATHER WAS back on the scene by now working up at the Ford Motor Company's Dagenham plant and so I got a job up there as an arc welder. But I was still only 19 and you weren't supposed to work there until you were 21. After a few weeks a guy came up to me with a sob story saying that his wife had had a heart attack and he needed to do day work would I mind doing a spell of nights for him? I said I didn't mind swapping for a while but after a month of it I'd had enough: working nights I couldn't go out and sing and this bastard wouldn't swap back. It was driving me nuts.

Well, Dagenham docks was just down at the bottom of my lane so I thought I'd pop down and see if they had any work going there. As I turned the corner I see a bloke standing at the bus stop and I offered him a lift. It turned out he was going to Samuel Williams, which was the lorry firm at Dagenham docks, so I said 'Well jump on.'

After I dropped him off, I parked up the bike and asked at the gate if there were any jobs going. The fella told me to go and see the personnel officer, who just happened to be the bloke I'd given a lift to, and he said, 'What are you after?'

It turned out the only job vacancy was in the oil farm, loading tankers and so forth. I knew nothing about it but I said I'd have a go. I gave in my notice at Ford and a week later I started at Samuel Williams.

The docks were good to me. The unions were strong and you could get up to all sorts. The boats used to arrive and you could buy bottles of gin for a pound and stuff like that, and of course being the enterprising guy that I was, I started a little trade in alcohol and everything else I could get my hands on.

Also in Dagenham docks they used to have what they called the coal fields, where they would unload the coal. Coal was very expensive to buy at the time and naturally we had a coal fire back at Sunnings Lane. I'd sold me motorbike and side car by now and bought myself a Ford. The back seat used to lift up and of course whenever I used to go over the coal fields I'd lift up the back seat, fill it up with coal and take it home.

I once had a whole barge load of salmon away. I didn't actually physically nick it but I put the barge where someone else could. Because rationing hadn't long ended there was a ready market for pretty much anything that we could get our hands on.

I was a right little thieving bastard to be truthful, but a lot of us were. We were a proper bunch of tea leaves. There was one fella we used to call Batman cos he couldn't go home without Robbin'. It was common to nick 500 gallons of diesel. I needed to because I had kids around me. It was a way of life. Everyone turned a blind eye to it. I even had a Customs officer take me to one side and ask if there was any chance of me getting him a bottle of Scotch.

I was working on the oil installation, the boats used to come in and we'd unload them. I learnt to drive a crane and, after a little while, I became jetty foreman. Being the foreman was great because I could do whatever the fuck I wanted to. But it meant I was responsible for the jetty.

One day we had a boat coming in called the *Good Gulf* that needed to have so many hundreds of tonnes of oil unloaded from it in a certain time otherwise it would have settled on the bottom. So we've got all the cranes up in the air with all the pipes ready so that as it landed we could bolt it up, the tanks were empty and they could start pumping straight away.

So I'm standing there with a crew of fellas and I could see this *Good Gulf* coming up, and I said to them, 'It ain't half coming up fast.' All of a sudden it started to turn and I thought, that's never going to be able to turn in the time that it's got, so I just turned round and shouted to everybody: 'Get off the jetty!'

And of course the jetty was 50 or 60 yards long so everybody started to leg it. I stood there until the very last minute and then I scarpered and of course the boat hit, and it ploughed itself into the jetty a good 15 foot. Crunch!

The impact was so great it actually moved the offices which were on shore. Anyway, I was in charge of the jetty and there was this boat stuck 15-foot into it, so when the managing director of Samuel Williams, Mr Carmichael, came huffing and puffing along I was the one he wanted to talk to. He could see the cranes and everything else and it was obviously all completely buggered now. He asked for the foreman. I stepped forward, and Carmichael said, 'Did you see this?'

'Yes, I did sir,' I replied.

'Well, what did you see?'

'I saw this big boat coming up the river, guv, and I said to the boys, "He's coming up too fast," and when I see him starting to turn I thought he's never going to be able to swing that boat round 'cos he was coming in at high tide and I told everybody to get off the jetty.'

Carmichael shook his head. 'And what steps did you take?' he asked.

'Big 'uns,' I replied. 'And fucking plenty of 'em!'

Well, he didn't think that was funny at all. I got a reprimand over that, and I was suspended for two days even though the collision had had nothing to do with me and I'd probably saved some lives or at least saved men from injury. But all Carmichael was worried about was that the jetty was out of work. People were replaceable, profits weren't. And profits were all he cared about.

*   *   *   *

I was always singing in the docks, because we had the tanks there that we kept oil in and if you sang in them when they were empty you had the best echo system that you ever heard. And the other blokes always made me feel good with encouraging words like, 'He's only fucking singing again', 'What a fuckin' racket!' and 'Put a fuckin' sock in it, Albert.'

All the time I was working in the docks, I never stopped doing my cabaret act. Every other night I'd be out singing and whistling in different pubs all around the area and the East End, only now I would slip in the odd joke between the songs.

The blokes I worked with were a funny crew. One was called Phil the Pram 'cos his wife was pregnant every year. They were all nice enough guys and we had a great time but they were all married and most of their wives were at work too, and none of them wanted to do Sundays because that was the only day they could have with their missus. So I always used to volunteer to do the Sundays 'cos they were a doddle. On a Sunday you had to load ten, maybe 12 lorries. You'd go in at 8am and you'd be finished by midday. Plus you got double time for working on Sundays. So it was a result. And then I'd have Mondays off 'cos my wife was at home with the kids.

But even though I was doing them all a favour, there were complaints made because I never worked on a Monday so I got dragged in front of Mr Carmichael again and he said, 'I notice you have quite a lot of Mondays off.' I said, 'That's right, I have sir', so he said, 'Is there a reason for it?' I said 'Yes, I don't mind working for double time and having single time off.'

'What do you mean by that?' he asked. I said, 'Well, have a

look down the list at all the blokes who are moaning about me, none of them will do Sundays, I'm the only one who will come in on a Sunday, so I work Sundays and have Monday off. But you give me double time for Sundays, so I don't mind working for double time and having Mondays off.'

He thought about it and he said, 'I've got to tell you, I make you right but I've got to be seen to be punishing you, so I'm going to put you on four days suspension with pay, starting from today.' And he told me to go back to my locker, pack and tell them I had the four days suspension but not to mention that he was paying me.

So I went back to this lobby and I said to the crew, 'You bastards have just buggered up this job. Because of your moaning and groaning, Carmichael will now go to shift work and he will do a seven day a week shift, and that will bugger you up completely.' And lo and behold, less than a month later he brought in shifts: 6am-2pm, 2pm-10pm, and nights; which meant that I had to do night work again which inevitably interfered with me going out singing, and I knew that it would be the beginning of the end for me and the docks.

CHAPTER FOUR
ENTER JIMMY JONES

ONE DAY I was working down at Dagenham docks and there was a phone call for me from Bob Wheatley, the publican, offering me a full time job. It was 1960 and I was 22.

Turned out the Royal Standard at Walthamstow were looking for a compère as they'd just sacked the old one, a very good Cockney comic called Charlie Smithers. I wasn't working that night so Bob invited me along to try out and offered me the job permanently. I decided to try it out for a couple of weeks first.

That first week was fine as I was working the early shift, but the second week I was working 2-10. Obviously I couldn't be in two places at once, so I had to be a bit crafty. I decided that I'd go to work at 2pm as I was supposed to, but at 7.30 I'd do a runner and drive over to Walthamstow to do the show. Then I'd either come back at 11 or get somebody to clock me off. It was perfect. I was getting away with it, too, but there was one guy on the crew who was very jealous of me. His name was

Roy Finch and he's dead and buried now, the dirty, no-good, grassing bastard. He knew what I was doing and he set out to drop me in it.

Finch wanted to get me the tin tack and he came up with a cunning plan worthy of Blackadder's mate Baldrick to stab me in the back. He went up to the management looking all concerned and told them that I had gone missing and that he was worried in case his good friend Albert had fallen in the Thames and drowned. It was Oscar-worthy stuff.

That started a panic and the management sent out people to look for me. They were so convinced I was brown bread they were talking about draining the dock to find the corpse. But before they did someone had the bright idea of phoning my Grace indoors on the off-chance that I was there. Grace played dumb of course. Luckily, she knew exactly where I was and what I was up to.

She phoned me at the Royal Standard and told me what was going on, so I came hurtling back. I was there by 9.30. It was pitch black and I came in by way of the coal fields. I grazed my head purposely and rolled in the coal dust. I looked a proper state and came wandering into sight like a zombie. The guv'nor demanded to know where I'd been and I simply said that I'd seen a guy nicking petrol and I chased him over the coal fields and that I'd fallen over, hitting my head and knocking myself out. I'd only just come to, I said.

They could see the cut on my head and the blood so they took me straight over to medical. I'd gone from been a slippery no-good AWOL bum to a local hero. And Finchy was gutted. He couldn't do anything about it. He just had to wipe his mouth and put up with it. But of course I couldn't carry on with this double life – I was supposed to be working nights at the dock the following week. I couldn't get away with it again.

I went back to Lou Wheatley and explained my predicament. The laws of economics came into play. I was earning £21 a week in the docks, but the Royal Standard was offering me £23 a week to work for them. Two quid made a difference back then, so it was problem solved. I went back to the docks and handed in my resignation. They didn't even ask me to work a week's notice either, which was handy.

And that was how, in 1960, I became a full-time, professional entertainer.

I still had to take a drop in money initially, however, because up until then I had my wages from the docks plus the regular £8 a week I was earning as a semi-pro. Before I turned pro, I'd been working four nights a week at the Romford United Servicemen's Club and I had my own backing band – Peter Gresham on piano, Don Bishop on drums and Peter Thornett on bass. I did Thursday, Friday and Saturday lunchtimes and Sunday night for £2 a session.

On top of that I lost all the perks of being a docker – all that handy access to black market gear. Apart from anything else I had to buy my own petrol now, whereas before I was having at least a couple of gallons away every day.

Within a week of going pro my name was changed to Jimmy Jones – but not by me. I'd taken over the Royal Standard gig from Charlie Smithers and Don Harvey from the resident band, the Don Harvey Trio, used to keep fucking up my name on stage. He'd been introducing Charlie for so long that instead of calling me Albert Simmonds he would introduce me as Albert Smithers. After seven days of this I'd had enough of him getting it wrong and he said, 'Sorry, Albert, we're going to have to change your name.' That night he went on stage and to my surprise he introduced me as Jimmy Jones. He said he'd done it in honour of Tom Jones because I sang a bit like him and that was it – Jimmy Jones was born.

At first I was a singer who did a couple of gags between songs, but I had a good memory for gags and if I was on a bill and the comedian didn't show up I would do his spot for him. A few of the comics on the London stag circuit were impressed with my delivery and my cheeky face, especially Pete Demmer and Ronnie Twist. It was the same time I had the previously mentioned bad throat and was drinking a bottle of port and brandy a night to help it. My doctor told me later that this had the opposite effect; it was actually knitting my vocal tissues together. I ended up having my tonsils out and then my adenoids. It was almost as if nature were intervening to say, stop singing, be funny.

From that moment in 1962, I switched the act around and instead of being a singer who told gags I became a comedian who sang a few songs. Ronnie Twist was really encouraging. He got hold of the sheet music for the Tom Jones song I sang called 'Help Yourself' and he added across the top of it 'to my gags'.

He told me I could use his act, but he said, 'Remember where you steal a gag from, if you nick a gag from any other comedian, remember who and where, because it's a small circuit and you will run across that act somewhere some day and you don't want to be doing their act in front of them; you need to find your own voice. Find your own way of using the material. Make it your own, and then you will become a comedian.'

And that was the best advice anyone ever gave me about comedy. With Ronnie's words ringing in my ears, I was away. I nicked a bit of his act, nicked some jokes off of a couple of others until I had enough material. All I really learnt was how to interpret the jokes in my own distinctive way.

At first I did mostly silly gags. I did Irish jokes, like the Irish fella who bought himself a ladder and had to put 'stop' at the end of it. What is stamped on the bottom of a bottle of Irish beer? Open other end. How do you burn an Irishman's ear? Phone him up when he's doing the ironing. Did you hear about the Irish woodworm? It was found dead in a brick. And what about the Irishman who had a boil on his arse and stuck a plaster on the mirror?

There are hundreds of them. We had a lot of Irish in the pub at the time and they loved Irish jokes, they loved laughing at themselves. And of course they used to do the same kind of jokes themselves about Kerry men.

I never wanted to do topical comedy, or satirical stuff. My comedy was all about sauce. All I ever wanted to be was another Max Miller. I never wanted to offend – I wanted to offer people an escape from their everyday worries. They come in and see my act and they forget about their gas bill or the leaky taps or whatever disaster was in the news. They have a bloody good laugh and they leave the pub or the club or the theatre feeling better in themselves.

Soon I was adding jokes of my own, developing the accents and adding filth. The Jimmy Jones the world knows had arrived.

Here's Neil Warnock, later my manager for more than a decade, on the secret of my success: 'Jimmy Jones may have started with a borrowed act, but what he had was an amazing ability to hear a gag and embellish it; he would grow it into a whole routine, connecting it to other stories, going off at tangents then coming back to the gag to round it all off. That was his expertise; that's what made him different. He would hold an audience in the palm of his hand and he could take them anywhere. And he knew how to work softer audiences – he knew how to take the material to the edge of what was acceptable, gauge the reaction and then come back. He'd get a few gasps, but no one ever walked out.'

CHAPTER FIVE

WHAT A KRAY DAY

I FIRST MET the Kray Twins in the early 1960s. I was still at the Royal Standard and I was doing a bit on stage when this guy came in and gave a nod to the drummer, Eric. He got down for a Jack Dash – a slash – and they had a few words. Afterwards Eric said to me 'You ain't got plans for later have you? Only we're working tonight. Don't ask questions.'

Well, he took us to the Regency Club in Stoke Newington, which billed itself as 'North London's smartest venue'. It was an illicit gambling den with a cellar bar. Eric had his wife Stella with him, and I was with Grace who was pregnant with Peter at the time. It turned out to be a command performance, but not a royal command; more East End royalty. Both of the Kings were in attendance, Reggie and Ronnie Kray, and the 'Queen Mum' was there too, their mother Violet. The club was full of villains. It was an audience you couldn't refuse. And one you wouldn't want to disappoint.

Once we were in the club, we heard the metal security doors

clang shut behind us. It was ominous. I remember thinking, Fuck that, this must be what it's like to be banged up. But obviously in a luxury prison because they had two bars and women were allowed in. You wouldn't want to upset the screws, though.

Lenny Peters, who later found fame as half of Peters and Lee, was on piano, Eric was on drums, George Watkins was on bass, and we had a sax player whose name escapes me. I was singing and telling gags. We played from midnight until 2am, two solid hours. Drink was flowing, they was all up dancing. Afterwards Ronnie came up and thanked us personally and gave us all a drink. He slipped a £10 note in my top pocket, the equivalent of about £150 today, and at the time, I was still working for £21 a week for eight sessions. *£10!* I'd never even seen a cockle before. Back then you could buy four pints for about five bob (25p), so it was a nice drink. For £10 you could have taken a girl to Southend, had a plate of cockles, some whelks, a couple of pints, fish and chips, tried your luck on the train and if she was any good booked into a bed and breakfast... and still have had change.

Ronnie was surprisingly softly spoken and easy to chat to. He was particularly happy because Violet had taken a shine to my singing. He shook my hand, looked at Grace, smiled and then he told me to take 'Mum' upstairs for a Chinese on the Firm. He sent Les Burns up ahead of us to tell them to keep the restaurant open for him. We'd never even seen Chinese food let alone tasted it. So we went up and tucked in to this exotic new grub while Lenny stayed downstairs playing. It was quite an evening.

Lenny Peters was incredible, a remarkable man. Very bright. He used to run with the Krays as a kid. The story was he'd lost his eyesight after colliding with a barbed wire fence. But he got me out of London one night: I was lost and Lenny managed to direct me from the Power Box Club to Tottenham Court Road from memory.

Anyway, Violet Kray had enjoyed the set so much that she wanted more and, before I left, Ronnie said, 'You'll be back next week, Friday and Saturday.' I wasn't asked, I was told!

I ended up doing the Regency Club once a month for over a year. It was full of notorious faces. Even when the Twins didn't have a financial interest in the place they always got in there. All of the faces would be in there: Ronnie Hart, Tony Barry, Chris Lambrianou, Freddie Foreman, big George Dixon from Canning Town. Through Reggie and Ronnie I met Barbara Windsor and her husband Ronnie Knight at the Astor Club, and Danny La Rue too.

At the club I'd sing ballads that were in the charts, and I carried on performing for them off and on until the Krays were sent down in 1969. Violet particularly liked the songs of Tom Jones and Engelbert. Her favourite song was 'The Last Waltz', so I always did that for her.

At the same time as I was a regular at the Regency Club I was still doing the Royal Standard, too. We used to have a priest come in, Father Knight from Bethnal Green, and he'd get up and sing and then pass his box around. He sang one night when the Krays were there and he appealed for donations because he had no Christmas presents for the kids in the orphanage. The following day a lorry-load of toys arrived. They were from the Krays. I have no idea where they got them from but it's a sure bet they never paid for them.

There was nothing wrong with the Twins. In my experience they only hurt other villains and they looked after their own. I never saw any trouble in their club, nothing untoward, and they always treated the turns well. I still got the occasional 'Royal Command' when they were banged up. I was at Broadmoor one night, entertaining the staff, and I got the message: 'One of our inmates wants to talk to you.' It was Ronnie, of course.

I had a bit of a charmed life when it came to London's villains. The lot north of the river thought I was from Bethnal Green in the East End, so I was one of their own. In South London villains associated me with Peckham and New Cross, when in fact I've lived my entire life in Rainham, Upminster and Hornchurch in Essex. So you could say I've got away with murder – but not in the same way they did.

I worked for the Richardsons as a singer first, before my time at the Montague Arms and after I'd got the sack from the Royal Standard. They had a pub called The George in Lambeth Walk, and I was doing regular spots in there for them, singing and telling jokes, from 1962. They had another place in Lewisham called The Cat's Whiskers, and two or three clubs. I didn't know they were villains at first – they were always very kind to me. They saw some of my late night shows.

Later on, when I was being managed by Neil Warnock, I got a call from Charlie Richardson asking me if I'd work for him and I asked if he'd mind doing it through Warnock as that was the way it had to be with Neil – everything had to go through him. I'd just assumed he'd know who the Richardsons were.

Well, Charlie called Neil and said he was a friend of mine and asked him about the gig he wanted me to do. Neil asked him for the money a month up front. Charlie said, 'You do know who you're talking to, don't you?' Neil replied, 'Yeah, Mr. Richardson.' He had no idea. Now this could have gone one of two ways, and luckily for Warnock, Charlie was tickled by it. He told him, 'I'll tell you what I'm going to do, I'm sending the money around now with one of my men, but you'd better be there on the night.'

Of course, when Neil told me about the conversation I had to explain who the Richardsons were. They were known as the Torture Gang – a charge Charlie always denied. The colour drained from Neil's face. On the night a rather more sheepish Warnock came along, half-expecting to have his toes removed with bolt cutters, and instead Charlie shook him by the hand. He'd just wanted to meet the man who'd had the balls to ask Charlie Richardson for money up front.

I continued to work with some of England's most notorious villains without upsetting anyone until one night at Caesar's Palace in Luton when there was a noisy fella with a beard at the front. He was annoying me so I steamed in to him a bit. 'Cor,' I said. 'Are you wearing a mask? You're an ugly bugger you are. You look like a parrot peeping through a hedge, mate.' I turned to the woman he was with and said, 'I'm surprised your guide dog hasn't 'kin' bit you.' Then I turned back to him, and went on: 'I do apologise sir, I shouldn't have come out yet; I should have let you finish eating that squirrel first.'

It wasn't until later that he came backstage and introduced himself that I realised what I'd done. That noisy gentleman was Wilf Pine, the only English villain ever to have been made a made-man by a New York mafia crime family.

He put his arm round me and said, 'Jones, if you hadn't been so fucking funny I would have jumped up and smacked you. But as it was you're a hero and I fucking love you.' I got away with it!

I got away with it with Roy 'Pretty Boy' Shaw as well – he took it off me, but I don't think he'd have taken it from anyone else. On one occasion when a fight broke out in the audience at the Circus Tavern, I stopped the show, and the bloke throwing the punches was Roy. 'Roy,' I said, 'Are you a friend of mine?' He said, 'Of course I am, Jim.' So I said, 'I wouldn't dream of coming to one of your boxing matches and starting a fight in the crowd while you were in the ring. Now, I don't know what this fight is about but please sit down and let me finish the show and then afterwards if you still want to take it further you can take it outside in the car park. But if you don't, I'd like you both to come to my dressing room for a drink.' Well, they stopped and they came back after and neither of them knew what they'd been fighting about.

The only real trouble I had at a show was also at the Tavern, and it involved a local villain called Kenny Tyler, now deceased. A fight broke out, so Kenny pulled out a Jif bottle full of ammonia and sprayed it at a fella. It missed him and hit a woman. The police were involved. They came backstage and asked me what I'd seen. I said, 'Nothing, there was a spotlight in my face.' And what had I heard about it? 'Nothing, officer.' And they believed me. I could never be a grass, but I used to dread playing the Tavern when Kenny was there. He'd always come backstage and would never leave until the entire drinks cabinet was drained.

There was an incident once at Bailey's in Hull. I was working at a country club down by the prison. The one night I had off, I got Frank Carson to cover for me. Frank walked on stage and a fight developed right in front of him; a proper, big ding-dong. Frank stopped talking and watched the fight, then he looked at the audience and said, 'You can't beat a good fight, good night!' and he fucked off. It was a classic line – and the only way to deal with it.

This happened in 1973, just after the film *The Exorcist* came out. I remember that distinctly because Frank's new joke at the time was about the fella who didn't pay his exorcist and got repossessed. These days of course exorcisms are different. Now you have to pay the devil to come in and take the priest out of the child.

I did quite a bit of charity work for the police as well. In 1976 a cop called Nicky Moore asked me to do a benefit show at the Dorchester, but I already had a gig booked in for that night in Hackney. The only way Nicky could get me from Park Lane back to Kingsland Road in time was in a squad car with the sirens going. As we raced through the East End a lot of people clocked me. All the herberts assumed I'd been nicked!

The Dorchester show went well except, before I went on, Eric Morecambe sat down behind me with a pipe and said, 'I bet you won't say "Fuck it" tonight, Jonesy.' I'm saying, 'Turn it in, you bastard,' because I was trying to memorise the gag order but he kept on baiting me. Eric was a very nice man. He got up and did about an hour-and-a-quarter after I'd finished, and you had to feel sorry for Roger De Courcey because he had to follow him.

After the Montague Arms, one of the pubs I worked in was The Eagle at Tottenham which was right next to the police station, but owned by a villain. I'd never seen an audience like it – cops and villains mixed together. One particular day PJ Proby came in The Eagle to see me with a problem. You didn't have to see PJ to know he was there, you just had to smell him because he always reeked of garlic. Proby's problem was that he hadn't had his passport stamped when he'd come into the country and was worried that he was going to get deported. A friend of mine called Stan Snell had The Ship in Folkestone which used to have a lot of immigration officials drinking in there. I made a phone call, Stan made a call, and one of his regulars had Proby's passport stamped so it said he'd come in via Dover. Problem sorted.

CHAPTER SIX

WHAM, BAM, THANK YOU RAM

RUSSELL BRAND ISN'T the first performer to realise how sexy a comedian can appear to an audience. I've had many come-ons over the years but the most extraordinary thing happened at the Walthamstow Royal Standard. I went in to the gents and this guy came in, a hulking great Irish man, stood alongside me, and asked if I'd seen him with his wife. I had, because she was gorgeous. He said, 'My wife would like you to make love to her.' I didn't say much, just, 'Very nice.' He went on: 'I'm quite prepared for this to happen providing I can sit there while you do it.'

He worked at Ford Motor Company at Dagenham, and I used to go round and service his wife, who was English, on a Thursday night once every three weeks when he was on days. He would sit and watch with a face like stone. All he ever said to me about it was, 'If ever I find out that you've been around here behind my back I will kill you.'

I agreed to that and asked him why they'd wanted me to do

it. He didn't say anything; he just unbuttoned his fly and showed me his cock which was like a button mushroom. Half an inch smaller and he'd have been a lesbian.

'All I want is for my wife to have satisfaction,' he said flatly.

I don't mean to boast but I have no problem in that department. I'm not saying I'm big but when women see it for the first time they don't know whether to suck it or feed it a bun. No wonder his missus was pleased to see me.

I carried on servicing her for about six months after that, always at their house in Downham Way, and always with him there. I was tempted to see her when he wasn't there, but he was a big fella and when he said he'd kill me I think he 'kin' meant it.

At the end of the six months he said I wasn't to come round any more. I turned up at their door and he said, 'Not tonight, she's pregnant. It stops now.' Pregnant! It could well have been mine, I didn't know and they wouldn't say. And they never came back down the Royal Standard. I never saw them again but she was fucking lovely and I enjoyed every minute. And if that Holly Willoughby is reading this and likes the sound of it and wants to break in more of her shoes, I can fit you in every other Thursday.

There was a lot of shagging back then. I was known as the Ram of the Royal Standard. I was knocking off the governor's sister Barbara, who'd used to date Don Harvey. But when she decided she was going back with Don to be a proper couple she told me I had to start shagging her sister or else she'd get me the sack.

I had another two sisters at the same time one night, Sandy and Rachel. I went back to their place… lovely girls. They looked alike and if memory serves they even licked alike.

One night the singing legend Dorothy Squires came in, she'd had a couple of hit singles by then and had broken up with her husband, Roger Moore. She was a good friend of the Wheatleys who ran the place, but for some reason she took offence with me. It must have been my mannerisms, because I wasn't telling gags then, but I was very cheeky, so I went to apologise to her and we ended up going out. This must have been 1964. I ended up spending the night at her mansion in Bexley, Kent, on a couple of occasions. I'll never forget her bedroom because it was the first time I'd ever seen a round bed.

Ten years later the place burnt down. I bet the bed caught fire. She was quite a goer for an older woman. Three of her songs were 'I'm In The Mood For Love', 'Anytime' and 'A Lovely Way To Spend An Evening' – which pretty much sums it up. She had a fabulous voice. She was in her late 40s then and she liked a toy-boy. Edna was her real name.

I first met my second wife Marion at the Royal Standard. She came in one night and turned every head in the place. She was stunning: big breasts, blonde hair, big arse, long eyelashes. Lovely. I was immediately told by the governor's wife 'Keep your eyes off of her', and Marion was warned off by Barbara who told her: 'Keep your eyes off of the Ram!'

Marion was not an easy conquest – it took me a month, although she says it was three months – to get her into bed.

She was 18 at the time. I was 28, ten years older than her,

but I told her I was 25. And I think the only reason she went out with me was that I had been sterilised – a story I'll get to shortly. She never wanted kids, but she did help raise some of mine. Marion came on holiday with us for 20 years, which may sound strange but it suited all of us for Grace to turn a blind eye.

My wife knew about Marion for a long time. She put up with it because Marion was doing something that Grace did not want to do. After she'd had six kids, she shut up shop. Sex was out the window. She told me flat, 'That's it, I don't want it anymore.' I said, 'Well what do you expect me to do? Do you want me to live like a monk?' She said, 'No, get it where you like.'

Even at our divorce she admitted that she'd known about my girlfriend for 34 years. Not that it stopped her taking me to the cleaners. I always told the kids, I did not divorce your mother, your mother divorced me.

Marion wasn't from a showbiz background and at first she found it all a bit hard to take. I took her to see her first strip show at the Regency in Tottenham. We were back stage and one of the strippers walked in, Maureen Grayson, and I played with her tits for a couple of minutes. Marion was flabbergasted. She couldn't believe what she was seeing. But we were like that all the time, there was nothing really sexual about it.

Carol Lee Scott (who became famous as Grotbags the witch on kids TV) was the same with me. She'd come backstage and say 'Come on, Jim, give us a look at your willie. Swing it around a bit for me.' Marion was mortified. But Carol loved seeing my dick, because I am blessed in that department. I think that's what turned her face green. But it was all harmless fun and it was part and parcel of the entertainment business.

I'm not sure if that argument would stand up in court, but the cock still would.

Newlywed couple, both virgins, have gone back to her mother's for their honeymoon night. She cooks him a lovely meal and then her mother says, 'Take him upstairs now, I'll do the pots and pans.' So they're upstairs and they're stark bollock naked except he won't take one of his socks off. The young bride tries to take it off but he won't let her. She says, 'But you said tonight I could see you naked.' He says, 'I am naked, you can see me nudger, can't you?' But she's not happy, she grabs the sock, pulls it off and sees that half of his right foot is missing. The bride screams and runs downstairs. 'Mum, mum, mum,' she says. 'He's got a foot and a half.' Her mother says, 'Right. You do the washing up, I'll go and sort him out.'

*   *   *   *

While I was still at the Royal Standard, my wife Grace fell pregnant for the sixth time. She was supposed to be on the pill, too. I went to the doctors and asked if we could sue the people who were manufacturing it and it turned out that Grace had the pill but wasn't taking it. Hence she was pregnant with the sixth child.

The doctor came up with a solution. There was a charity

organisation back then called the Simmons Population Trust who would pay for married men to be sterilised if the circumstances were right. I made an appointment to see a specialist called David Wallis in London, up by Finchley, and my wife and I went up for a consultation. He asked to see our marriage licence and explained that if I went ahead with the operation I wouldn't be able to father any more children. My attitude was if anything ever happened to my kids, God forbid, I wouldn't want to start again anyway.

He looked at me, nodded his head, and said, 'Yes, I will do this.'

I said, 'When am I going to have this done?'

'Now,' he replied.

My arse went all over the place. It's one thing making an appointment and other thing to submit to surgery just like that. But he was nonchalant about it. It was an everyday occurrence to him.

'Right,' he said. 'Go into the next room, take your trousers and underpants down to your knees and just sit there.' He didn't even buy me a drink first.

In the room there was a black reclining chair like you'd see in a dentist's. I sat there with my crown jewels on display and Mr Wallis came in and wheeled this trolley in front of me. It was full of lots of different bits and pieces, including scalpels and knives.

I have to confess that when it comes to operations I am a wimp, a very big wimp. I can't stand the sight of blood as a general rule and if it's my blood I'm really bad. This wasn't going to be easy.

Casually, he moved my knob over to one side, picked up a needle and gave me an injection in one of my testicles. At this point, I was laying back and not looking at what he was doing but he sliced open the testicle he'd anesthetised, gone inside it and pulled out a tube which he cut. I know that every male reader is wincing at this point, but imagine how I felt!

Then he got a little electric soldering iron, seared both sides, put it back and stitched everything back up. Four stitches it took, and that was it. Now for the other bollock. He moved my knob over the other way and cut into the other testicle but he'd forgotten to anesthetise it. I screamed with pain.

'Oh, I'm sorry about that,' he said. And he injected me quickly.

I said, 'What is this place, the 'kin Nutcracker Suite?' and he laughed.

'You haven't come on a motorbike have you?' he asked.

'No.'

'You haven't come on a horse?'

'No, doc, I've come by train.'

'Well, when I'm done get yourself home very carefully.'

I left his practice with a lump of cotton wool either side of my nuts. Walking back to the station wasn't too bad. But of course it's quite a long train journey from Tavistock Lane, where his offices were, back to Essex. By the time we had got to the other side of Mile End the anaesthetic had started to wear off and as the train started to rattle a bit – boompety-bom, boompety-bom – the pain was unbelievable. Talk about great balls of fire.

We finally got to Upminster station where I'd parked the car, and now I've got to drive home. Everything I did – pressing down the clutch down, working the accelerator and the brake – was absolute agony. My nuts were in a terrible state. Somehow I managed to get us both home, but I realised there was no way I could drive myself up to work that night in Walthamstow. So I phoned the bass player, John Bishop, and he came and picked me up, but of course everybody at work was killing themselves laughing about it. Jonesy's had his nuts done, the Ram's been gelded. You've got to remember this was 44 years ago and it was uncommon back then. I was a pioneer – of pain.

Before the show I was sitting in the stall singing, one of the songs that was a hit at that particular time was 'Young Girl' by Gary Puckett And The Union Gap and as I went for the high note I felt a stabbing pain down below. Somehow I'd split all the stitching and there was blood trickling down my leg. Oh, Puckett. We managed to patch it up with cotton wool but after that I came home. There was no way I could risk performing and splitting them again.

I went to my local GP the following morning, but he told me I had to go back to the specialist. I phoned up Mr Wallis and when I told him what had happened he said, 'Just rest.'

The Royal Standard gave me time off to recuperate, but of course while I was resting I wasn't earning, and to make things worse my nuts swelled up and turned black. Everyone laughed at that, even Grace. The only one who didn't laugh was me. I was in 'kin' agony.

It took weeks before my nuts went back to the size they were supposed to be. They looked like a Christmas turkey.

That wasn't the end of the story either, because Mr Wallis had told me that I should have as much sex as I could manage for the next six weeks and even masturbate as much as possible to get all of the healthy potent sperm that I'd produced out of my system. Now, personally, I don't mind wanking, you meet a very nice class of person. So I did what I was told.

After the six weeks were up I had to go back to see him so he could make sure I was infertile. I either had to bring my sperm up in a bottle or he said they'd take a sample. The thought of me going back to Tavistock Place and having some dolly nurse give me a J Arthur appealed to me immensely as you can imagine. But my missus wasn't having any of that. 'No,' she said. 'You'll take it with you.' So after the six weeks, I went back up there with a bottle full of fresh sperm in my pocket – it wasn't a pint bottle, no, it was only a small one.

When I got up there, the nurse was an absolute darling and I thought to myself, dear oh dear if she's doing a J Arthur, I'll keep quiet about the bottle and have one. There was only one bloke in front of me. He went in to a room with her and came out with tears in his eyes.

'What's the matter mate?' I said.

'I thought I was going to enjoy that,' he said. 'You go in and she tells you to drop your strides. But to take it off you the doctor comes in and puts his finger up your arse. He touches something up there, your knob goes splosh and they take your sperm from there.'

When this dolly nurse came out I just said, 'I've got mine in a bottle here.'

Mr Wallis tested the sperm and I was then declared sterile. Since then, I've been a Jaffa: seedless. I'd never make my wife pregnant again, nor anyone else's wife either.

A week after the sterilisation was official, I went to confession. The priest said to me, 'You have broken the rules of your religion and from this day you are ex-communicated.' I still sent my children to Catholic schools though.

Fella goes to the doctor's, says he can't get a hard-on. So he sends him to a specialist who has a good look at his tackle and says, 'I know what the 'kin' problem is here, son, your left nut is defective.' The fella says, 'Can you do anything about it?' 'Yes,' says the surgeon, 'I can give you a transplant.' So he sends the nurse down to where they store the left testicles and as luck would have it they had one left in stock. Well she gets a pair of tweezers and picks it up but as she starts to walk back she trips and the little nut rolls all the way along and down a drain. So she says to this other nurse, 'What can I do? I need a left testicle and that was the only one left.' And her pal says, 'Well nip into the kitchen and get a pickled onion. It's about the same size and he'll never know.' The nurse does this and she tells the specialist what has occurred. 'Don't worry,' he says. 'It's all psychological anyway.' So he does the operation and tells the fella to come back in six weeks time. Six weeks later, he's back and the surgeon asks if his ker-nob is working again. The fella says, 'Well yes and no.' The specialist says, 'What do you mean yes and no?' And he replies, 'Well when I'm with my wife nothing happens, but every time I see a cheese sandwich...'

I had another painful incident some years later with bunions. It was winter 1982. I had bunions on both feet, and had them removed all at the same time. Four weeks later I went to have the stitches out but the night before I'd gone to see Jim Davidson at the Circus Tavern and Jim had got me pie-eyed. I'd fallen asleep with my boots on and in the morning I couldn't get them off. I'd gone to see the surgeon and he came at me with a great big 'kin' saw. As soon as I saw it I was up and out of the room. He was only going to saw the boots off but I thought he'd have my foot off.

A fella goes to the doctors. He gives him a proper going over and says, 'I've examined you and I can't find anything wrong with you. You must have Alice.' The fella says, 'What's that?' The doctor replies, 'I don't know, but Christopher Robin went down with it.'

*   *   *   *

When the time came for me and the Royal Standard to part ways it was a bit of a drag – literally. And the TV star Dick Emery was to blame. It was a Monday night, Dick was the star booking and the place was absolutely packed to suffocation. It was £3 a ticket too, which was a lot back then.

We started the show at 8pm and the phone rang at half past. It was someone wanting to speak to me. It was Dick Emery.

'What's up, Dick, are you lost or something?'

'No I'm in France, we were filming *The Dick Emery Show* and I was due to fly home but it's got very foggy and I'm not going to make tonight.'

'But we've got a pub full of people here ready to see you.'

'Well I'm terribly sorry, I just can't make it; I'm not going to be there.'

He didn't sound that sorry though. I asked him what we could do about it, and he told me that Lance Percival was available. It would have been more surprising to hear of a night that Lance Percival wasn't available. I politely declined the offer and asked if he could get Bruce Forsyth to step in for him. 'Oh no,' he said. 'Bruce wouldn't do an East End pub.'

I said, 'Well in that case we'll have nobody – we'll do it without you.'

Which explains why I ended up on the stage, wearing women's clothes and a blonde wig, and doing Dick Emery's act. Yes, the truth can be told, Jimmy Jones was a drag act – for one night only.

I went out and did everything that I'd ever seen Dick Emery do on the television, including Mandy, the 'Ooh, you are awful' girl, and honky tonk Clarence. And we gave all the customers the opportunity of either going to the bar getting drinks worth £3 or going to the door and changing their ticket and getting their three quid back.

Believe it or not, only 22 people took the money, the rest of them spent it over the bar. I thought it was a success, but Lou Wheatley had died and we had a new pub guv'nor called Al Morgan who rang me up the next morning and sacked me.

I thought I'd done him a favour by dragging up and standing in but he blamed me for Dick Emery not turning up. Thanks, Dick. I never believed he was stranded in France. He either bottled it – Emery suffered terribly from stage fright and would often throw up before a performance; his skin came out in blotches because of it – or he was off getting his end away somewhere because he was a lecherous bastard. He married five times, every one of them a showgirl. And he left the last one for another showgirl, Fay, who was very pretty and 30 years younger than he was. It wasn't unheard of for Dick to drive hundreds of miles after a show just to dip his wick.

He hated other comedians, hated them, especially any of the Cambridge Footlights lot, who he called 'pampered Jessies'. And now he'd fucked up my regular gig at the Standard. Suddenly I was out of work with a wife and six mouths to feed.

I rang a comedian friend of mine, Rob Maynard, who told me to drive straight up to Manchester and said he'd get me work straight away. I rang him at 2pm, got to Manchester at 6pm and good as his word I was on stage that night as compère at The Wookie Hollow in Liverpool. The top of the bill was Tommy Cooper.

Their regular compère had gone sick so I did Tuesday, Wednesday, Thursday, Friday and Saturday for £25 a night. Bearing in mind I was working at the Royal Standard for £28 a week, this was an absolute result. Plus The Wookie Hollow was a fabulous venue, it was the first place I'd ever worked which had a glass stage. I had never performed to Scousers before, and they were a great crowd. I was a fresh face from London telling jokes and singing and they took to me, which was lucky because they could be wicked bastards if they didn't like you. Dustin Gee died up there. One fella kept shouting 'Get him off' all the way through his routine. Frustrated, Dustin turned on him and said, 'You're ruining my act, can't you say anything constructive?' And the Scouser shot back: 'Meccano.'

As well as The Wookie Hollow I was doubling up. I'd come off stage in Liverpool at 11 and shoot back to Manchester to go on stage at midnight at the Del Sol in Manchester, which was full of entertainers who went there to drink after their own shows. I did four nights a week there, for £20 a pop. What a week. I'd never seen so much money.

I drove home overnight and got home at dawn because we had been due to go on holiday on the Saturday. We went to the seaside town of Walton-on-the-Naze on the North Essex coast; we were a day late but it didn't matter because for the first time ever I had a stack of cash in my pocket. It was absolutely wonderful. We stayed at a caravan site, the beaches were golden, the kids had a fabulous time.

My wife told me that a fella called Charlie Palmer had been round to see me and wanted me to call him, so I rang him on the Sunday and he wanted me to work the Elm Park Hotel in Rainham, Essex, on the Saturday night after we got home, and the Sunday lunchtime and the Sunday night all for £25 a go. I was replacing Mike Reid who had had to go abroad suddenly for reasons I won't go into. So suddenly I was earning £75 for three sessions. Dick Emery had gone right up in my estimation. And after the first weekend I got the Friday nights as well. I had a good band too, led by a fella called Steve Liddle.

Charlie did try to change my name to Billy Budd, but I never liked that so I stuck with Jimmy Jones. Everything was fine for a few months but then they had a problem. Charlie had promised Mike Reid that he could have his old job back when he came home, but he didn't want to lose me. So he offered me Mondays, Tuesdays, Wednesdays and Sunday lunchtimes and gave Mike back the Fridays, Saturdays and Sunday nights – Thursdays were out because that was jazz night.

This suited me, and so I carried on working the Elm Park Hotel for the early part of the week, and moved on to The George in Lambeth, which was owned by the Richardsons, for the weekend gigs. After a few weeks, I was approached by a fellow called Maurice King from the Mary Arnold Organisation, a big London agency, who asked me to compère a Sunday night show at the London Palladium. Top of the bill were a band called Blackwater Junction. Every performer wants to play the Palladium and so I leapt at the chance. Before I went on stage, they took me to one side and warned me that if I uttered so much as one swear word they would drop the curtain in front of me. Well, I was as clean as a whistle but what was funny was John Bouchier the ventriloquist was in the first half and clearly nobody had had the swear word talk with him because his puppet, Charlie, turned the air blue. He was a great vent, though. He made Charlie recite tongue-twisters like Peter Piper Picked a Peck of Pickled Peppers.

We also had a very classy Scottish singer called Benny Yorke in the first half, and it went very well indeed. But then Blackwater Junction did the second half of the show and before they were finished, there were more people outside in Argyll Street than was left in the theatre. They were louder than an air raid, they really were.

That night was one of the stepping stones in my life. After that the trickle of people wanting to be my agent and manager became a flood – but I'll deal with that later. Most of them were full of easy promises but you can't feed a family on pie in the sky.

CHAPTER SEVEN

KINNELL!

I NEVER USED to swear on stage, I would use the catchphrase 'Kinnell!' which I always explained was short for 'blinking hell' – and I'd add 'you can please yer 'kin' selves if you 'kin' believe me or you 'kin' don't.' I actually got the idea from watching a football match on the telly. I'm a big Tottenham fan and Spurs were playing Sunderland when this particular player missed a penalty for the Mackems. His name was George Kinnell and as he missed you could hear the shout go up from the Sunderland fans: 'Oh Kinnell!' And I thought I 'kin' like that!

What a brilliant line for a catchphrase.

I wasn't the only one to think that though.

'Kinnell!' was mine, I thought of it and everyone knew it was my saying. But back when I had a residency at the Montague Arms in South London I was also working the Pontin's camps – Camber Sands and Pakefield, near Lowestoft in Suffolk. There was a young man there working as a comedian who I thought was very funny. His name was Roy Jay, and one day he showed up at my house. He'd got the sack from Pontin's for thumping the bar manager and he asked if he could come and work with me as a warm up. He had no work and nowhere to stay. I felt sorry for him and moved one of my children out of their bed so he could sleep at my house.

I took him to Yarmouth but when I pulled up at Pakefield the security guy on the gate said, 'Is that Roy Jay you've got in the car?' I said, 'Yeah,' and he said, 'He can't come in here; he's barred from all Pontin's camps.' So I had to take him in to Yarmouth and get him an evening's bed and board while I worked the camp. He was pot-less. He didn't have a penny on him, so I gave him a bit of spending money too.

But when I got back to Pontin's I found out the story wasn't quite what it seemed. He hadn't been sacked just for thumping the bar manager, it turned out his girlfriend was also working behind the bar and got caught helping herself to drinks. So I knew I couldn't entirely trust Roy. But he was a good comic and I didn't like to see him in trouble, so I picked him up, drove him home and phoned Bob Wheatley, and got Roy working as a comedian for the Wheatley Organisation. Roy ended up doing the Circus Tavern at Purfleet, the Windmill at Copsford, and lots of other venues, because Bob had so many pubs and clubs in those days. He also spent a week sleeping at my house and gigging around and he earned quite a lot of money from that.

Shortly after he disappeared up North, and three weeks later the word came back to me that he had changed his name to Roy 'Kinnell' Jay. What a 'kin' liberty! I was furious. After all I'd done for him, this was how he repaid me? I didn't mind someone stealing a few of my gags, but this was one of the unique parts of my act. He really was taking the piss.

I immediately went up Yorkshire to sort him out. He was appearing at Batley Variety Club where he was opening for Shirley Bassey. I drove up there, paid for my own tickets on the door and went in. I was still seeing red; I was going to have him.

Somehow down the line the word got back to him that I was in the club. And when he finished his act he came clean. He said, 'Ladies and gentlemen, I'm ashamed to say I don't deserve your applause. I stand before you as a thief. I nicked all of my act from a guy down South and he's paid me the compliment and privilege tonight of coming up here to watch me. He's over there; ladies and gentlemen, put your hands together for the legendary Jimmy Jones.' And I thought, what a clever boy, now how can I bollock him after he's done something like that? We became friends again after that and he sensibly decided to drop the stolen 'Kinnell' from his name and become plain old Roy Jay again.

Some people will remember him by the name he adopted later: Roy 'Slither' Jay. He used to come out on stage dressed as a convict and say 'Slither hither' and 'Spook!' He got his big break in the 1980s when Chic Murphy, who used to manage The Three Degrees, got him a £1 million TV advert deal with Schweppes. He recorded a couple of them but was then found coked-up on an ad shoot and he was deep in the *shh... you know what*. Schweppes cancelled his contract. Chic was furious and Roy, who always liked to get legless, ended up with all of his limbs broken.

He was last heard of living over in Benidorm working the clubs, but sadly he died in December 2007.

CHAPTER EIGHT

IT'S A ROYAL KNOCK-OUT

I NEVER EXPECTED to entertain royalty, not with an act like mine, but I became a royal favourite by accident.

Progressive rockers The Nice, forerunners of Emerson, Lake & Palmer, used to come and watch me in South London pubs in the late '60s. There was Keith Emerson the keyboardist, Davy O'List the guitarist, drummer Brian Davison and Lee Jackson the bassist and singer. They blended rock, classical music and jazz; they were very talented boys, and they happened to be big fans of what I did. And it was their idea for me to open my own room at Gullivers nightclub in Down Street, Mayfair, just along from the Hilton Hotel. The owner had a disco upstairs that did good business but he also had a downstairs room that was hardly used.

The Nice took me up to meet him and at their suggestion he turned it into the Kinnell Room. I appeared there Monday to Fridays. I never went on until half-past-twelve, one o'clock in the morning; but it caught on. There was a buzz about the place and we'd get a lot of people in there. There were people in the entertainment business, celebrities and sportsmen who I'll get to, a lot of very, very rich Americans who were in London at the time, and a lot of wealthy Jewish teenagers who all seemed to have flash cars.

There was one section of the room that was always kept in the dark and which would be patrolled by some very tough looking men. It turned out that this section of the room was reserved for royalty, and it was kept dark so they couldn't be photographed drinking or doing anything else indiscreet. Sometimes I wouldn't be able to go on until 2am because the club had got the word that a royal guest was coming in and the show would be held up for them. Princess Margaret saw me a lot; she liked a tipple I can tell you. Philip came in, and so did Prince Charles. In fact, the only one who never came in was Her Majesty the Queen. I don't know why. It can't have been my language – it wasn't any worse than Philip's!

I performed for the royals on several variety bills, not the Royal Command Performance itself, but I entertained Prince Charles and Princess Margaret at charity functions. Charles came and spoke to me before the show when we did a fundraiser at the Circus Tavern once. He shook my hand and said, 'Now Jim, will you be doing anything off the records?' He meant my Kinnell vinyl albums which we used to knock out at the Montague Arms in the 1970s.

I said, 'I'd like to Your Highness but I'm afraid the organisers have banned me from doing the blue material tonight because you are here.'

'Don't worry on my account, Jim,' he replied. 'You won't offend me; give us the good stuff! I've got all the records!'

He was disappointed when I explained that I had to stick to my brief.

'Well,' he said, 'I hope you're not going to use cue cards like the fellow I saw last night, Bob Hope. I read the punchlines to every joke before he reached them.'

I didn't use cue cards and I believe his Highness had a good laugh even without what he called the good stuff.

A while later, in the late '80s, I did Blazer's at Windsor and the manager was perturbed to see some people coming in from Windsor Castle. He went up and warned them that Jimmy Jones was an x-rated comedian. One of these fellas, an equerry, replied: 'I know, but if Prince Charles can drive around with his tapes in his car I'm sure he'll be fine for us.'

Princess Margaret came to the Circus Tavern too, on another occasion, but the good stuff she liked was Famous Grouse whisky which had to be served to her poured into a teacup from a tea pot so the punters wouldn't realise what she was up to. I got on very well with Princess Margaret. In fact one of my only royal disappointments involved her.

We had a royal charity show lined up, down at the Kings Club in Eastbourne in the early 1980s. I was running a nightly variety show down there at the time and was expecting to perform for her on that occasion, too, so I was disappointed when the owner broke the news that the top of the bill had been in and watched me and they wanted me off. I won't say who they were because they're still alive and it might cause bad feeling, but I can assure you that it's true. He came in, saw me, and said: 'He's too good a singer to be a comedian and too good a comedian to be a singer, I don't want to have to follow him. I can't have anyone as good as that on the show.' So I was off the bill. I still went along anyway, and I met Princess Margaret backstage.

'What a shame you weren't on tonight,' she said – in front of the top of the bill. 'I was very disappointed; I was looking forward to seeing you again.'

My show at Kings was called The Jimmy Jones Show. I worked with an impressionist called Tony Maiden, we did four nights a week then, and Sunday lunchtimes; and we always sold out. So we decided to stretch the show; we got a band in called Triple Cream and I auditioned and found a dance troupe called the Lovers. I also had the privilege of giving a start to a very funny young man, a mimic called Bobby Davro.

Shortly after we filmed my first ever adult comic video there, *Live At Kings*. The club owner paid for it, because they saw it as an advert; we used three cameras and recorded it over two nights. It sold 275,000 copies and it's still selling today.

As well as the stealth royals, a lot of showbiz names and sporting celebrities came in to Gullivers too. All of Hot Chocolate used to come in and see me, including Errol Brown, the singing Malteser. George Best was a regular. John Conteh the boxer would come in at 3am after he'd been running around Hyde Park and I used to sit upstairs with him after my show and have egg and steak with him. We became close friends indeed.

*   *   *   *

The miners' strike of 1972 almost killed me. Literally.

I was driving back along Oxford Street after performing at Gullivers nightclub. The lights at the junction with Regent Street were on green, so I went straight across. Unfortunately the lights on Regent Street were also on green – it was some malfunction caused by the power cuts. Well, this fella in a Triumph TR2 sports car came straight into me. The copper who saw it all said he was doing 60. My car, a newish yellow Datsun 160A, was a write-off. When they had it in the breaker's yard the next day, they couldn't believe that anyone could get out of it alive.

The centre door post ended up right in the middle of the car. I smashed my head on the windscreen. My girlfriend Marion in the passenger seat was thrown right on top of me. And my passenger ended up with a broken collar bone. She was Ayshea Brough, a singer, an actress and a TV presenter – she hosted a pop show called *Lift Off* which became *Lift Off With Ayshea*. She was an exceptionally beautiful girl. Poor Ayshea was in agony, but she said, 'I can't be seen to be here,' and so she got out of the car and flagged down a taxi to take her home.

Never mind lift off with Ayshea, this was fuck off with Ayshea.

Ayshea was married to Archie Andrews' son Chris Brough at the time and he didn't know she was out. He thought she stayed in on a Friday night oiling her hair. In reality she was sneaking out to see my show and to meet up with Roy Wood, who she worked with. Anyway she couldn't be involved in any adverse publicity so she fucked off.

No one was nicked because the copper who witnessed it all knew that both sets of lights had been on green. His mate who turned up later wasn't much help. He said something really stupid: 'Had an accident have we, sir?'

I said, 'No, mate. I'm a stunt driver, you've just mucked up a shoot.' Daft bastard.

So I then had to get a taxi to take Marion home to Tottenham and then me home to Essex. 6am I eventually got in.

We'd had a very lucky escape.

This happened on the Friday night, and on Sunday I was appearing at the Palladium. I had nothing broken but I was shaken up and in a lot of pain. Luckily one of the punters at the Montague Arms was a doctor called Rodney Pell, and I went to see him at the Medway Hospital where he gave me acupuncture to ease the agony. He very kindly came to the Palladium on Sunday and did the same before my act and took the pain away.

I had another problem though. I was still working Gullivers – only now I didn't have any transportation. A stripper friend of mine called Maureen Grayson heard about my plight and lent me £600 to buy a new motor. She had a very kind heart. And fantastic tits. I paid her back, of course. Thanks to her and Dr Peel I never missed a show.

And Marion and I stayed friendly with Ayshea. By the way,

she'd played a character also called Ayshea in the Gerry Anderson science fiction TV series *UFO* – and after that incident I found out what the *UFO* stood for.

*   *   *   *

I decided I wanted a duo in to work with me at Gullivers. I had a pianist called Ted Taylor but I needed a drummer. My musical director, a fella called Billy Day, reckoned he knew a good one called Michael, so we had him in for an audition. He was a great drummer but he was also bloody loud. When he was playing downstairs in the Kinnell club they could hear him upstairs in the disco *above* the sound of the records. So inevitably we were getting complaints. I had to tell him either you learn to play quieter or we'll have to find a different drummer. He tried his best, he put dusters and stuff on the kit, but he couldn't keep it down – he said, 'That's the way I play, Jim.' So I had to give him the tin tack.

He came back about ten years later to see me. I was appearing at the nurses' quarters at Whipps Cross Hospital in Leytonstone. And he said, 'Do you remember me? I've brought my band over to see you.'

That man now used the nickname Billy Day gave him – Nicko. You might know him better as Nicko McBrain, and his band were called Iron Maiden. Well, I'd never heard of them but they seemed a nice bunch of lads. They were local boys from Leytonstone and Hackney, and were very down-to-earth. I gave him and his band all my goodies, my comedy cassettes, and that was it.

The next morning I was so chuffed about seeing them I rang up my manager Neil Warnock to see if he could help them get a deal because he was involved in the rock side of things through the Bron agency, which he ran. There was a moment of silence on the other end of the phone. Finally Neil spoke.

'You know Nicko McBrain?'

'Yeah, he used to drum for me. I sacked 'im.'

'You *sacked* Nicko? And he brought Iron Maiden down to see you?'

There was a note of incredulity in his voice.

'Yeah, I thought you might be able to give them a leg up.'

'Jimmy, Iron Maiden are the biggest heavy metal rock group in the world. Their albums go in the UK chart at No 1, they've had hits in America, they're massive in Europe and Japan...'

'Well they could have 'kin' said!'

Later, I found out that they played my tapes and videos on their tour buses, and mentioned me in their book. I had no idea who the fuck they were. I told Nicko and he pissed himself. We're still friends to this day. I do like heavy metal, as it happens, especially the lead off a church roof.

East End punk rock band the Cockney Rejects turned out to be fans as well. I met their singer Jeff at the book launch for Garry Bushell's novel *Two-Faced* in the West End a few years ago, and he said they used to come and see me at the Circus Tavern. They're out of Custom House and they're nice guys but they're a bit too 'kin' loud for me.

Promoting my Bournemouth show in the 1980s – it was nice of stripper Louise (left) to keep her clothes on.

Above: Kinnell – a bestseller! With my manager Neil Warnock and lovely Linda Nolan. She gave me the gold disc; I wanted to give her a pearl necklace.

Below: Me and Dave Lee with two Flying Squad detectives after doing a show for their autistic children's charity.

Above: Live on stage at the Starlight Rooms, Enfield.

Below: My grandsons Mark and Tommy – born on the same day (17 February 1982) in different hospitals.

Above: With Jim Davidson in my garden at Four Oaks, Upminster.

Below: Here I am at BBC Radio 1 with DJ Simon Bates. Was he Smashie or Nicey?
I don't remember.

Backstage at the Circus Tavern with Chubby Brown (I taught him how to swear!) and the venue's owner and former pro-wrestler Paul Stone.

Above: Plying my wares.

Below: A boxing dinner for the Nordoff Robbins music therapy charity (to my left is Neil Warnock; two people to my right is Simon Porter, now Status Quo's manager).

Left: My son Paul on his wedding day and, right, his best man David.

Right: It's Grotbags! Me with Carol Lee Scott – what a grot she's got.

A publicity photo.

IT'S A ROYAL KNOCK-OUT

There are these two punks and the fella is about to slip the bird a right length. He puts on some backing music and reaches for a condom. The bird says, 'Here, is this Johnny Rotten?' He says, 'Nah, I've only used it twice.'

CHAPTER NINE
THE FULL MONTY

'Jimmy Jones is to the Montague Arms as Sinatra is to Vegas' – Frank Durham, journalist, 1971

THE MONTAGUE ARMS doesn't look much. It's a medium sized pub in Queens Road, at the New Cross end of Peckham, South London. But it's the venue I was most associated with in the 1970s when 'Jimmy Jones' became a byword for a whole underground comedy scene. Everyone from rock stars to apprentice comedians, and lords to villains made a pilgrimage to this homely-looking old-fashioned boozer, just a bottle's throw from Millwall's Old Den, with its live music, its blind keyboard player, its strippers and me.

I was involved with the Montague from the start. One Monday night I was working at the Elm Park Hotel in Rainham, Essex, when a couple of Northerners called Peter and Stan approached me and asked if I was interested in working their pub in Peckham at weekends. They offered me

Thursday, Friday, Saturday and Sunday, and seemed quite keen. It sounded good, so I drove over and had a look at it. To be honest, it was a khazi. At that time, they didn't even have a stage, but it had potential.

Peter Hoyle, the owner, was a drummer and Stan, his brother-in-law, was his bar manager. They had a fella called Mel on the piano, who was a decent singer and quite a good organist. On my advice they built a stage; Peter did some fantastic alterations with the help of the brewery and the Montague Arms was re-born as a venue. They listened to me and I got them to put on acts who knew how to work that kind of pub crowd.

We would have strippers on Monday and Wednesday nights, and Sunday nights we'd put on drag acts. And it took off really quickly. We'd be banged out most nights. The fire limit was 200, but we regularly packed 300 in. You couldn't fall over in there, there was nowhere to fall.

Lorry and taxi drivers spread the word; it was them who turned me into a word-of-mouth sensation.

I had a guy come in one night whose name was Bill and who said he was a bassist. We hit it off and became instant friends. I didn't know who his band was, and even when he brought them down I was none the wiser. I didn't recognise them. There was Bill, Charlie, Keith... better known as Bill Wyman, Charlie Watts and Keith Richards. All of the Rolling Stones came down, except for Mick Jagger. And I always used to chat to Bill and have a laugh. But all I really remember about them is that they were big beer drinkers and they loved my jokes.

I had no idea I had rock star fans. I first met Paul

McCartney at a charity event for Nordoff Robbins, the music therapy foundation, in the late '90s. Paul just came up behind me and jumped on my back! He said, 'Jonesy, it's a pleasure to meet you. The Beatles used to play your tapes on our tour bus.' Another revelation. Linda was with him and she said, 'Even I understand your humour, Jim.'

Back at the Montague, Peter Hoyle noticed that there were more and more punters coming in just for my comedy routines. And he had a very bright idea. 'Wouldn't it be nice,' he said, 'if we had something to sell all these lorry drivers who are spreading the word about you.' What a great idea. No stand-up comedian had ever released a vinyl long-player of adult material before. So we recorded *Live At The Montague Arms*, released on the Montague Arms label. It was very popular, we sold thousands of copies of them in the pub. Bill Wyman certainly bought a copy. We finished up recording five stand-up LPs from the Montague Arms, and I haven't even got a set of them myself, but I'm told they make a lot of money nowadays on the second hand market and eBay.

One night another young man came down to see me. I can see him now, skinny young bastard with gingery wavy hair. He was from Blackheath. He said he was a drummer but he wanted to become a comedian.

I said, 'Are you old enough to drink, son?'

'Not really,' he replied. 'But I like a pint.' And he downed his beer in front of me. His name was Cameron Davidson, better known as Jim, and he was hungry.

'How do I become a comedian, Jimmy?' the kid asked.

There was something about him I liked, so I gave him a copy of whatever albums I had on sale at the time and I told him what I had been told many years before: take what you want from my act, but always remember where you got the gag from and make it your own.

I gave him the albums and he went away, but I didn't give him his talent, because Jim Davidson is a very talented man. Difficult and self-destructive maybe, headstrong certainly, loyal definitely, but talented beyond question. Jim has got a fantastic comedy brain, he is a natural story-teller, and his impressions are spot on, too. Two years later Jim was performing at the Montague himself, although the Adam & Eve was where he really got started. Two more years after that he won the TV talent show *New Faces* with the 'Nick Nick' joke he'd nick-nicked from another London comedian, and the Chalkie voice. A star was born.

Just after he shot to fame, Jim Davidson and I took part in a Battle of The Comics down the Old Kent Road in South London. Bob Todd from *The Benny Hill Show* was the referee. It started with me at The Dun Cow and Jim performing at The Green Man, which was directly opposite. Then we changed pubs. I met him in the middle of the road and said, 'What of my stuff have you done, Jim?'

'All of it!'

We stood there for a quarter of an hour trying to work out what jokes we could still use. The night ended with both of us together on stage at The Dun Cow. Now, both the pubs had been rammo and for the last bit all of The Green Man punters had to force their way into The Dun Cow. It was a wonder no one was crushed. It made the average Japanese rush-hour train look roomy.

The funniest thing from the night though was Bob Todd. He was steaming out of his box when he got there and was on the sauce all night. The next day I took a call from Bob's wife asking if he'd stayed the night with me. He hadn't even gone home! He finally turned up three days later in Belfast and he had no idea what he'd been doing, how he'd got there or why he'd gone.

Jim Davidson wasn't the only would-be comedian who came in to see me at the Montague. A little later, another older guy did the same. He had a thick North-East accent and I gotta be honest with you, I thought he was a lorry driver, I really did. He was a big strapping fella, over six foot tall and quite burly. He saw a couple of the shows and came up to me for a chat after one of them. His name was Roy and it turned out that he was also a drummer who wanted to become a comic. He told me that he was in a band up North, and that his manager had asked him if he wanted to be a clean comedian and be one of thousands, or if he wanted to be an outrageous comedian and be one of five or six.

Roy told his manager, George Forster, that he wanted to be an outrageous comic and stand out from the crowd. 'Who should I see?' he'd asked. And George Forster turned round and said, 'Go down and see Jimmy Jones.' To which Roy's words were, 'Who the fuck is Jimmy Jones?' Only he pronounced 'fuck' as *fook*.

Forster told him to get himself down to London, jump in any black taxi and ask the cab driver to take him to see Jimmy Jones. That's exactly what he did – and the driver dropped him off outside of the Montague.

He stayed in New Cross, he came down the pub every night for a week and he bought all of my records. At the end of that week, away he went. I didn't even ask his full name, which turned out to be Royston Vasey. Although of course you'll know him better as Roy 'Chubby' Brown, the monster of mirth he became after studying at the Jimmy Jones school of comedy. Roy was very soon re-born as Britain's rudest comedian. Years later, he told me: 'You're the reason I am who I am today.'

And again what a talented guy and a nice person as well, we're very good friends to this day.

By the mid-1980s, we found ourselves in similar situations. Chubby was a big name everywhere north of Birmingham, while I was selling out venues all over the south. There was talk of a joint national tour, but it never came off. Then George Forster wanted to put the two of us on together at the Hammersmith Odeon, but he wanted Chubby to get the majority share of the box office so Neil Warnock blew it out. Eventually Roy became a fully-fledged national icon under his own steam anyway.

When I first signed with Polygram to do my videos, they asked if I could recommend any other blue comedians. I gave them Chubby's name and number. It was on my recommendation that they signed him up. *From Inside The*

Helmet came out in 1990 and he's put out a show every year on video or DVD since.

*   *   *   *

The Montague Arms represented fabulous years for me. Some of the strippers – Jack the Rippers they were called – were absolutely sensational. Others were just shocking. One was called Annalette, a lovely-looking woman but her husband used to turn up while she was working and he'd sit in the audience and have a J Arthur. He got turned on by the fact that she was getting the audience turned on. And she knew he was doing it, too. I had to stop him. I gave him a tug about giving himself a tug, and he was banned from the pub.

One of the black girls was very lithe indeed. She was called Samba and she used to come on stage with a big afro wig and a python. She used to do what I would call yoga moves. She'd put her foot behind her head and show the audience what she'd had for dinner while the snake coiled around her. Unfortunately, on one particular occasion as she brought her leg back from behind her head, she caught her big toe in the syrup and pulled it right off of her head. Everyone just fell about. Poor cow.

Everyone was terrified of that snake. No one would go near the dressing room when it was in there. She asked me to stand and hold her snake once, and I was very tempted to ask her to kneel and hold mine. We could have played a game of snakes and lather.

Years later there was another stripper who worked with a

python but she used to put a foot of it up her Jack and Danny.
I don't know what the snake made of it, but that's what I'd
call charming!

I suppose if she'd wanted it to finish her off she'd have used
one that rattled.

Not long after we got started we changed organists from
Mel to a blind fella called Peter London – his real name was
Peter Cook but he had to change it because Equity already
had *the* Peter Cook on their books. I believe he still works
there today.

The Montague Arms only turned sour for me when the
word got out that I was about to appear on the smash hit ITV
show *The Comedians*. This caused a lot of jealousy and then
one of the resident musicians found out that I was earning
more than double what he was on a week, and so he started
putting the knife in behind my back, too. Peter Hoyle started
resenting the nights I didn't work the Montague because by
then I was being offered better paid work elsewhere, and was
putting in acts to sub for me and they weren't drawing the
crowds.

The Montague Arms was basically the Jimmy Jones show
with the musical backing of Peter London and Peter Hoyle
and the odd stripper thrown in. That's what the punters
wanted. But Peter Hoyle knew that *The Comedians* was
coming my way and that other places wanted me now, places
like Caesar's Palace in Luton and Pontin's holiday camps,
which were paying much better than the Montague Arms.

Pontin's had come on to me and offered me two nights a

week – Mondays and Wednesdays – for £50 a night. So I put other acts in to the Montague to cover for me, usually Tony Gerrard. I was getting a ton for working two nights at their camps at Camber Sands and at Lowestoft. This was very nice for me but Peter copped the hump about it. He didn't like me having nights off because every time I had a night off, he had a quiet night in the Montague.

So in his wisdom Hoyle decided that if I wouldn't give him 100 per cent commitment, then Jimmy Jones had to finish. And he did it on the phone which hurt after all those years. He said, 'If you're not interested in doing this job full-time I'm going to have to let you go.' It didn't make much sense to me, if the place wasn't busy when I wasn't there two nights a week, why would it get any busier if I wasn't there for the rest of the time as well? But I just said, 'All right Peter, if that's your decision, that's your decision.' Then I asked: 'If this is the end of our deal, what are we going to do about the royalty payments for the records?'

He said, 'You'll only get anything like that if you sign an agreement that you won't work within a ten mile radius of the Montague Arms.'

How ridiculous was that? Apart from the unfairness of what he was asking, an agreement like that meant I couldn't work anywhere in East London, North London, or South London, or North West Kent or South East Essex… it was a complete restraint of trade. Besides, as I pointed out to him, I didn't walk out on him, he had sacked me. There was no way I'd sign anything like that. Nor should I. He'd cut off his own nose to spite his face by ending our relationship, and was sitting on money he owed me from five LPs of my material. No one was buying those records to listen to the drums and keyboards. But Peter Hoyle wouldn't budge and it finished up that we were involved in a very nasty and expensive court case which – to be honest with you – neither of us won.

It was a terrible shame that we didn't part company as good friends. I'd helped him make a fortune and I'd been a good pal to him. Peter had opened a second pub, the King & Queen at Mottingham, Kent. I'd helped him do it up when he bought it and I opened if for him with my dear friend Dave Lee Travis, the DJ, and an act who became very close mates of mine, a dwarf cabaret act known as the Mini Tones – Kenny Baker and Jack Purvis who went on to be in Star Wars as R2D2 and a Jawa.

So Peter Hoyle and I faced each other in court. It was the most stupid decision I had ever made in my life, but I was so blinded by the injustice of the situation that I hadn't thought it all through. We had a judge with one arm, but the old bastard had all his wits about him because he dropped both of us right in the shit.

On paper it looked like I had won the case because Hoyle was told he wasn't able to manufacture any more of the albums. But all of the details of the money that was made in the Montague Arms came out in court and this one-armed judge made sure that all of the testimony found its way to the Inland Revenue.

I had been earning £150 a week off of Peter Hoyle, which

was a lot of money back then, but I had only been declaring £75 of it to the tax man. The other half was disappearing into the deep end of the Jimmy Jones black economy. To us this wasn't an unusual arrangement because pubs and turns were operating in a world where everything was cash. This started for me back with good old Charlie Cutbush – no one worked on credit in that business, they'd never heard of cheques or invoices. And in the entertainment game it was exactly the same. Venues would have two sets of books – the real one, which stayed private, and the moody one that they showed to the taxman. It was all strictly pound notes, no questions asked, and stick the profits under the floorboards.

Both of us had been honest with the judge about how much of a cash cow that pub was. We didn't expect him to grass us up! It taught me a valuable lesson in life: even if right is on your side, it often pays to sit around a table and talk rather than go to law.

Airing our dirty washing in court would come back and bite both of us very badly a couple of years later.

*   *   *   *

A businessman is in trouble with the taxman who tells him unless he pays £1000 immediately he's going to jail. The businessman said, OK, wipes his mouth and hands him a grand in used notes. The taxman says, 'Let me get you a receipt for that.' The fella is flabbergasted. 'What?' he says. 'A thousand pounds in 'kin' cash and you're going to put it through the books?

The worst part of my fall out with Peter Hoyle was yet to come. That heartless one-armed beak took all the info about cash payments and what was declared and what wasn't and turned it over to the Revenue. Tax inspectors then followed me without me knowing about it for nine months. They trailed me to and from gigs, to pubs and clubs, to the shops. They knew where I'd been and what I'd bought. And eventually I was hauled in front of a tax inspector. They kept me there in their offices in Romford for six hours, from 10am until 4pm, without offering me so much as a cup of tea. I had my accountant in there with me but he was as much use as chocolate fireguard.

Because Hoyle had dropped me in it over the undeclared £75 a week, they wouldn't believe a thing I was telling them. They even asked me about part-time earnings from when I was working at Samuel Williams back in the dock. Back then when I was singing with the band we used to get 30 bob (£1.50) a night between us, which we would put in a whip for our drinks. No one made a penny; we just had a good night out with our wives. They went over this again and again, the fella wouldn't believe it.

Then he said, 'At the Montague Arms you were receiving £150 a week and only declaring £75?' So I said, 'That's true but out of that £150 I was also paying the strippers, and the other artists.' And he said, 'No, no, no.' In the end I had to say to him, if you call me a liar one more time I shall thump you. But they are suspicious bastards by nature. One sniff of moody money and they're on you.

Three days later I was sent a transcript of every single word that I had said. I thought this is going to hurt, I was stuffed here. Stuffed like a Christmas turkey. And eventually they said I owed £9000 in back taxes plus fines which were being calculated. Four years later I was told I owed £65,000! That's £56,000 in charges and fees. I don't know who worked that out but I think they must have been schooled in economics by the Mafia.

It turned out that the tax inspectors had carried on following me for about a year and a half because when I went in to appeal they told me, 'You decorated your living room and bought ten rolls of paper at £10 a roll' – and then they produced the bill. They knew what I'd bought and where I'd bought it from.

They also knew that I'd recently moved to a lovely big house in Upminster called Four Oaks The Chase. Now I'd paid £68,000 for it but £40k of that was mortgaged. The taxman said that they estimated the house was worth £100,000, and that if I sold it, I could give them £60k.

Yes, maybe so, but then where would I live?

I had a new accountant by then, Alan Soraff – I'd had to pay £700 for all the paperwork – and he got to work on my behalf. I was lucky because in his covering letter to the taxman, the one-armed judge had written that I was an honest fool, and they accepted his version of the events. In the end I was hauled in to Somerset House for a bollocking for tax evasion and after a great deal of negotiation they agreed to take £36k as a lump sum in settlement on condition that if I did anything like this again I'd be in prison. The problem was I didn't have it. I could lay my hands on £16,000 but where could I get the rest? Even if I sold the villa I'd bought in Menorca it wouldn't be enough. So I had to borrow the rest off of Bob Wheatley, who by now owned the Circus Tavern – or so I thought. Bob told me he was lending me the money, it was only later that I found out he'd persuaded Charringtons Brewery to stump up for it. But at least now I could give my accountant a cheque for £36,000 so he could pay off the taxman.

A month later I got another tax bill – for the interest on the £36k while they were waiting for the cheque to clear. The cheeky bastards. Alan Soraff protested and they swallowed it.

I thought I was hard done by but from what I hear the taxman clobbered Peter Hoyle for a whole lot more – more than double what I had to pay.

By the time I worked for Neil Warnock everything was done on paper and above board, but in the early '70s it was every man for himself. In many ways we were the pioneers of self-assessment.

They say you can't take it with you, which is true, but why give it to the taxman? It was the Arthur Daley mentality. Still, I got a few gags out of it: I had a very successful business lunch with my accountant today, I said. He paid the bill, I kept the receipt...

CHAPTER TEN

MIKE REID, BETRAYAL AND *THE COMEDIANS*

ITV LAUNCHED THEIR hit series *The Comedians* in 1971. It was an instant smash. The idea was simple. The show, made by Granada TV, took comics from the Northern night club circuit into the studio, filmed them and cut the footage into a rapid-fire succession of jokes. The turns were referred to as unknowns but of course they'd been honing their acts on the circuit for the best part of two decades. Viewers loved it, and the show made stars of such greats as Bernard Manning, Charlie Williams, Frank Carson, Jim Bowen, Colin Crompton and Tom O'Connor. As a result they all found their fees shot up from £50 a night to more than £1000.

Trendy people now are a bit sniffy about *The Comedians*, some even calling it 'right-wing' but at the time it received rave reviews everywhere from *The Times* to the Communist *Morning Star*, whose critic described it as 'very, very funny', adding, 'please watch it'. The show wasn't right-wing at all, it was just authentic working class humour and as such it was equally well-received by the *Daily Mail* and the *Daily Mirror*. It was also voted comedy of the year by the TV Critics Circle and theatrical paper *The Stage*.

The Comedians was the brainchild of producer Johnny Hamp, whose granddad had been a music hall magician. The director Wally Butler came from a showbiz family background too, so they knew the business and, unusually for TV executives, they knew what made the punters laugh. It was a terrific show and it ran for 11 very successful series.

My old pal Mike Reid was the first London comic to appear on it and I was really happy for him. Mike and his wife Shirley used to come and see me every week at the Montague Arms. Naturally, the subject of *The Comedians* came up, and I asked Mike what the chances were of me getting on it. Good friend that he was, Reidy promised to have a word with Hampy for me. This went on for a year, and I still hadn't heard back a word from Johnny Hamp. So I thought I'd better take matters in to my own hands and do it myself. I started to phone his office but I could never get through to him, I could never get past his secretary, a lady by the name of Lucinda. Except for the time I rang up claiming to be Mike Reid – she couldn't tell our accents apart and put me straight through, but as soon as Hamp knew who he was talking to he said he'd ring me back and never did.

About three years after *The Comedians* started an agent called Jack Sharpe was bringing down some of the turns to appear in a live show called The North Comes South. I did a show for Jack and top of the bill was Colin Crompton, a weedy

Mancunian comic who would shortly become more famous as the gormless compère on an ITV spin-off show from *The Comedians* called *The Wheeltappers and Shunters Social Club* – Colin's job was to ring a bell and tell the audience to 'give order' and then make announcements from 'the committee' between the acts. His funniest moment was when he interrupted Ray Allen the ventriloquist halfway through his spot and said, 'Excuse me Mr Allen, we've had some complaints that they can't quite hear you at the back. Could you hold your dummy a little closer to the microphone please?'

Colin watched my act, and when I came off stage he congratulated me on how well it had gone. I took the opportunity to ask him how I could get to see Johnny Hamp. Colin thought about it, and then smiled and said, 'Jimmy, if you really and truthfully want to get on *The Comedians*, I'll tell you now, on Tuesday this week Johnny Hamp is rehearsing *The Comedians* in Yarmouth at the Britannia Pier and he will be there, I'm on the show and I know that he's going to be there.'

So on Tuesday I cancelled all my plans, went down to Yarmouth and I smuggled myself into the theatre. And there was the great but elusive Johnny Hamp sitting in the audience saying how he wanted things done. So I went up behind him and I said, 'So you're Johnny Hamp, I was beginning to think you didn't exist.' Startled, he spun around and asked who I was. I said 'My name, Mr Hamp, is Jimmy Jones. I've been trying to talk to you for the past three years and you've not taken any or my calls or replied to any of my messages. So one of the comedians on your show told me that the only way to get hold of you was to meet you down here in person.'

He smiled. 'I like it, I like it,' he said. 'I love a bit of initiative. What are you doing next Tuesday?'

'What do you want me to do next Tuesday?'

'I want you to be at Granada, in Manchester, to do an audition for me for *The Comedians*. I want 12 minutes from you, and I only want 12 minutes, nothing more, nothing less.'

At last! Trying not to look too pleased, I said I'd be there. And then almost as a parting shot, I told him that a great friend of mine had been asking him about me appearing on the show. 'Who's that?' he asked.

'Mike Reid.' His face was a picture.

'Well,' he said. 'Let me tell you one thing, Jim, if Mike Reid is a friend of yours, you do not need an enemy.'

The revelation hit me like a bucket of cold water in the face. Mike Reid, my dear, old friend, had been putting the knife in to me for years while cheerfully assuring me that he was doing the opposite. I must have looked stunned, not to mention confused. So Johnny Hamp spelt it out.

'Your so-called friend Mike Reid is the reason why you have never been up to do *The Comedians*,' Hamp said. 'Mike assured me, that "anything Jimmy Jones can do, I can do". He said you were just a poor imitation of him.'

The cheeky bastard! So that was the reason why Reidy used to come and see me perform as regularly as possible – he was taking my gear and doing it on *The Comedians*!

To be honest, I hadn't watched every episode of the show. I

had noticed Reid do a couple of jokes I did on a few occasions but out of naivety I'd just put it down to coincidence. It wasn't, it was out-and-out theft. I was fuming. I knew things like that happened in the entertainment business but I hadn't expected to be shafted so blatantly by a man I considered a buddy.

I was devastated, but undeterred. I went away and rehearsed a solid 12 minutes and, good as his word, when I got up to Manchester Hampy was there and watched my audition. There were eight comedians all trying to impress him, but I was the only one who did 12 minutes as requested. All of the rest did 20 or 25 or 18. None of them stuck to the instructions. And at the end of the evening Johnny Hamp came up and said, 'Thank you all very much indeed for coming but the only one I'm going to use is Jimmy Jones because he was the only one who did 12 minutes. When I ask for 12 minutes, that's what I expect. If I'd wanted 20 I would have asked for 20. You've cost me a great deal of studio time tonight for no reason.' It was harsh, I suppose, because some of those guys were good, but Hamp had a point. In television, time is money. Afterwards he took me to the bar and asked if I'd stay over and do another 12 minutes the next night.

'Certainly,' I said. And he told me: 'I want you to do everything you can in your black voice, even Irish stuff, turn it to black – that accent is hilarious.'

And so that was how I finally got to go in and record *The Comedians* with all the big boys. And when I say the big boys I mean the people that had been on it for three years and were now household name stars – the likes of Bernard

Manning, Colin Crompton, Bryn Phillips, Frank Carson, and a young fella called Russ Abbot, who'd come from the comedy group the Black Abbots. I wasn't fazed by their fame because I knew them all and I'd worked with them, but it was still an exciting moment.

There was a sweet surprise still to come, though. We were doing a rehearsal for the show in the canteen, and when I got there who should be there but my dear old chum Mike Reid. He took one look at me and his face dropped. 'What the fuck are you doing here?' he asked, sweetly.

I told him that Johnny Hamp had invited me along personally. Reid's face was a picture. He looked as happy as a bastard on Father's Day.

'Well, I ain't keen on that!' he said, and he stood up and marched off to have a row with Johnny Hamp. It was a good 'un as well – you could hear it from the floor above and, long story short, that was the last time that Mike Reid ever appeared on *The Comedians*. That same night he accused me of being a joke thief and I lost my rag with him and said that no, he was the joke thief, he was the one who had being coming down the Montague Arms and nicking my material and doing it on the show, and if he wanted to we'd go outside there and then and I'd fight him over it. I'm not a violent man, but I was steaming mad. Reid's bottle went because he had a yellow streak down his back so wide that if you'd have parked on him you would have got a ticket.

Later that evening Russ Abbot introduced me to the studio audience. 'Ladies and gentlemen,' he said. 'I'm going to introduce you to a thief, because last night this man stole the show and he's gonna steal the show again tonight' Out I went to do another 12 minutes, going heavy on the black voice, and the crowd went whoosh. They loved it. I came off and Bernard said, 'Jonesy, you tore the bollocks off 'em.'

Afterwards Johnny Hamp told me he wanted me back the following Tuesday and Wednesday. This was it, I thought. I'd arrived. My elation was short-lived, however, because Hampy went on to say that this series looked like being the last for the time being and that ITV were planning to shelve it for a while – which turned out to be the case, but only because Hamp wanted to concentrate on *The Wheeltappers and Shunters Social Club*.

My series of *The Comedians* was transmitted between January and March 1974 and after that there wasn't another full run until November 1979. They say as one door closes another one opens, but in my case as one closed the next one slammed straight in my face.

It was still an absolute pleasure making the shows, though. I did another two 12-minute spots the following week, and that next Tuesday was when I really got to meet Bernard Manning properly. Bernard was lovely, he really and truthfully was. But he was a bastard, too. Just before I went on he took me to one side and told me that I was speaking too fast, so I slowed down and Johnny Hamp was most put out. He asked why I'd done it and I told him that's what Manning had advised me to do. He said, 'Take no notice of Bernard, go back out and do another 12 minutes but go back out as yourself, Bernard's having a laugh.' I thought no more of it.

Manning was working that night at the Oldham Broadway and he'd invited me to come along and watch. To my astonishment, he walked out onto the stage and he did word for word the 12 minutes that I had just recorded for *The Comedians*. And then he looked over at me and said 'Not bad Jonesy, was it? I only heard you once.' That's why he'd told me to slow down! I pissed myself laughing and we became firm friends.

The next night, back at Granada, Bernard introduced me to the studio audience, with these words: 'Ladies and gentlemen, I'd like to introduce you to Mike Reid's ulcer.' It was lovely, absolutely lovely.

The worst problem I had with a Manning wasn't with Bernard, but with his youngest brother Frank, a singer who had a club in Newquay called the Embassy, just like Bernard's Manchester club. Bernard fixed it up for me to do a week there, Sunday to Saturday. The first night went great, but on the Monday I happened to get there early and just as I got to the top of the stairs I could hear this guy telling the same gags that I had told the previous night. I went in and there was Frank doing a half hour early evening spot with my jokes. I was livid. When he came off, I said, 'Frank, what are you doing? These are the gags I did last night.' He said, 'Oh, I knew I'd heard 'em somewhere.' The cheeky sod. So I had to change the whole act around; and as luck would have it I had quite a lot of material in those days so I managed OK.

Afterwards I said to him, 'You can't do this every night to me.' He could see I was angry so he promised he wouldn't do any more gags that week.

This was the type of things that happened to me all the time when I was trying to get known as a comic back then. There were more thieves and rogues in the entertainment business than you'd find banged up in Parkhurst.

The Comedians didn't get paid much – just £50 for every show we did. But of course it all paid off because for most of the turns, the exposure meant your money went through the roof. I was luckier than most – I got £50 and a hotel room for the night because I'd come so far.

Marion used to come up there with me. She was 23 at the time and gorgeous. She wore short skirts or hot pants and when she walked through the Granada TV centre you could feel the draft from blokes turning their heads to follow her legs. One of the fellas up there, a top TV producer, a very senior guy, pulled me to one side and said: 'What's the chance of me fucking her?'

I said, 'You ask her, but stand well back when you do.'

'I could put you on TV,' he said. 'I could make you a star.'

I just said, 'Go and ask her yourself. I can lay on other women for you; I've got strippers who do it all the time, but you're wasting your time with Marion.' And he was.

The big shock for me was how much rivalry there was between the comics. Bernard Manning was notorious for watching people in rehearsals and nicking their routine when it came to filming. They were all very competitive up there and they stole everything. Colin Crompton nicked Norman Collier's entire act.

Most of the comics used a cue board with all their punchlines jotted down on it. On one particular night, Bernard went on first and started the show because he had a gig that night and out of devilment he did all the jokes on Frank Carson's cue board. So then Frank came out and he did all the gags on Colin Crompton's cue board. When it came to Colin and they had to stop the show. Someone else had to go on instead.

I never put my cue board out till the last minute, but all the regulars did. It happened to the great Liverpudlian comedian George Roper when they were recording the series before. There had been a power cut and Hampy asked Bernard to fill in. Manning saw George Roper's cue card and did every one of his gags. George, still backstage, had no idea. He came out and died on his arse. After three gags bombed, the crowd started to shout 'Heard it!' and George twigged what had happened and walked off.

We got in trouble after the show one night. A few of us – me, George, Johnny Hamp and Brian Marshall – went on to a nightclub called Deano's where Scott Walker, from the Walker Brothers, was headlining. We went to see Cannon & Ball, who were opening for him, and naturally the place was full of women who come along for Scott Walker. He came on stage wearing Jesus sandals, the scruffy bastard, so we started taking the piss out of him. We got so many laughs the bouncers came over to throw us out.

The Comedians was good for me and I started to do a lot of gigs in the North on the back of it. Mostly they were stag shows – two comics and eight birds, four in the first half, four in the second (in the South it was the opposite, you'd have six comedians and only two strippers). Some of those strippers up there were dirty cows. I walked into the dressing room once and caught two of them going down on each other.

On one particular night I was working a place called the Riverboat and two of the strippers had arrived, but two were still on their way. So we started the show, I did the first 20 minutes and I've got one of these girls standing on the side of the stage, waving at me – a very attractive young thing she was as well, all done up in a nurse's outfit. I could see she was distressed so I got the band to play a number, while I went over to sort out her problem.

She grabbed my arm and said, 'I can't come out, I can't do the show.' She was close to tears, so I said 'Why can't you do the show?' She said, 'Well, my dad is in the front row and he thinks I actually am a nurse.' The dirty old bastard was right down the front and all, so I sent her off to find another girl to take her place, while I went back and did a few medical jokes. Like the one about the old fella – and I pointed at her dad and said he looked just like him – who was lying in bed with a pretty young nurse giving him the once over. She was lovely, blue eyes, blonde hair, pert breasts. This old boy leans forward and whispers in her ear, 'Give us a kiss, darling.' 'No,' she says. 'Oh go on,' he says. 'Give us a kiss.' 'No,' she says, even more firmly. 'Oh please,' he says, 'Just a little peck on the check.' 'No,' she replies. 'I shouldn't even be doing this...' And at the time I just made the 'five knuckle shuffle' sign with my hand, but now the punch line would be 'I shouldn't even be wanking you off.'

A fella called Georgie Webb was my manager at the time (see the chapter All That Jazz), and after one of the shows we went on to the Long Bar in Manchester. I was up at the bar, chatting up a dolly bird, and she was a cracker. She was funny, blonde, bubbly and very beautiful. We were getting along very well. But when she went for a tinkle, Georgie gave me a tug and said, 'I didn't know you were gay, Jones.' I said, 'Eh?' He said, 'It's a bloke! It's Bunny Lewis – the drag act.'

Well she came back and I asked her out right. 'Are you a bloke?' I said.

Bunny gave me a wink and said, 'That depends...'

*   *   *   *

I was hurt by Mike Reid's betrayal. I'd known him for some time – I'd first met him at the Walthamstow Royal Standard, when he was a Sunday morning guest comedian/singer. Well, I say singer, he used to come on and mime to songs and do a 20-minute stand-up bit. He was always a bit of a fantasist, he claimed that he used to work for the Twins but that was never true. He drove some of the minor members of the Firm about, and that was the extent of it. He didn't ever work for the Twins. But he did work double hard to shaft me whenever he could. Sad to say *The Comedians* incident was not a one-off.

In 1974, I was asked by a Southern Television producer to come and judge a Nurse Of The Year competition in Southampton. It wasn't televised nationally, it was a regional show, but it was fun to get paid to chat up flirty nurses and I had a great time down there. After the show I was talking to this particular producer and he started asking about my family. I told him I had six kids, four boys and two girls, and he said, 'I think I've got a children's television programme for you.' He told me all about it and told me he'd be bringing me back down to do a pilot, to see how I got on with it. I was delighted. After we'd finished filming, we drove back to London because Marion lived in Tottenham. We used to eat in a great Chinese restaurant called Yips. All of the acts used to get in there after their shows and this particular night I ended up on a table talking to Charlie Smithers, Mike Reid, Charlie Scott, Paul Tracy and a few others, and I was telling them about this TV show that I think I've got down at Southern Television.

The following day I had a phone call from the producer. He didn't sound too happy. 'Were you out last night in a restaurant, talking about the show that I offered you?' he asked. I told him I was. He tutted and said, 'I should have told you to keep it to yourself because you've lost it.'

Shit. I said, 'Well, I didn't actually have it in first place, but why did I lose it?' He replied: 'Well, somebody you were talking to got their management to phone the governors at Southern Television.' It turned out that Mike Reid's manager Tony Lewis had told them that if they let Reidy do that show he would let them film a special on another one of his acts; a very very big act... And that's how I lost out again. The name of the show was *Runaround*, which, as you know, started in 1975 and became a big hit with kids.

So once again I'd been stabbed in the back by a gentleman

who I'd once considered a family friend, a man who I'd given regular work to when he'd been struggling. I gave him Mondays and Wednesdays at the Montague Arms when I was going out and doing Pontin's, and I was paying him £15 a night, which went up to £30 a night. And this was how he repaid me.

What could I do? I'd lost the show – and any lingering respect I had for Mike Reid.

But still it didn't end. A fella called Len Tucker, who I'd met back in the days at the Kinnell Club in Mayfair, loved my singing voice, and in 1975 he got me to record 'Lovin You Ain't Easy' – written by Tony Macaulay – with an orchestra for Pye Records and I became a Pye artist.

'Lovin' You Ain't Easy' had first been recorded by the great English blues singer Long John Baldry, so it was an honour to even be asked to do it. My version was entered as a contender in the UK's Song For Europe Contest, but The Shadows won with 'Let Me Be The One'. I should have done a cover of that: 'Let Me Give You One.' But the single was a minor hit for me and I did appear on a Pye compilation album with Petula Clark and Sandy Shaw.

I was doing a lot of demo work in Denmark Street with Tony Macaulay at the time – I did everything I could back then because I had six kids and I'd just bought my first house in Chestnut Avenue, Hornchurch, Essex. Tony was a Pye producer and a huge hit writer, he'd written or co-written a string of chart hits like 'Build Me Up Buttercup', 'Baby, Now That I've Found You' and 'Love Grows (Where My Rosemary Goes)'. And we became good friends. He used to come over to the Montague Arms when I was working and he thought the comedy was great. He loved my singing so much that he wrote me a song for me called 'Sad-Eyed Romany Woman'.

Unfortunately for me, Mike Reid was signed to Pye as well, and he'd just got to Number Ten in the charts with a novelty version of 'The Ugly Duckling', which Danny Kaye had first sung in the 1950s. He went in the studio after me to work with my producer Terry Brown. He was recording a follow-up single called 'The King Is In The All Together.' Mike got to the studio as Terry Brown was putting the finishing touches to the mix of 'Sad-Eyed Romany Woman.'

Reid was impressed.

'That's tremendous,' he said. 'That'll be a big hit. Who's singing that?'

'It's Jimmy Jones.'

Whoosh. Reid hit the roof. He stormed straight in to the MD of Pye Records, Peter Prince, and said, 'You don't release that song by Jimmy Jones while I am releasing "The King Is In The All Together".' This was crazy. His single was a novelty comic song, mine was a romantic pop ballad. They weren't in competition at all. But he was a star artist and he had clout up there, so Prince agreed to shelve my song, and it was never released. Once again Reidy had stabbed me in the back. I don't know if my single would have been a hit, all I know is Macaulay had a bloody good track record. The only small consolation for me was that Reid's single flopped.

Later on, Mike joined the cast of *EastEnders* as Frank Butcher and it was the same story. One of the big star names has told me that the producers had wanted to cast me for a part and when Reid got to hear about it he put the kibosh on that too. I'm not bitter about it.

I don't know what Mike's problem was. He was a strange man, very paranoid, and he was always envious of me. When he'd started I'd been a big name on the circuit and he seemed to go out of his way to get one over on me. I was never like that. I always trusted people and I liked to think that there was no nastiness in the entertainment business but I've got to tell you, the rivalry between Reid and I disproved that. It didn't bother me, I didn't care and I didn't hold it against him. I really do mean that. There's not a bad bone in my body and as far as concerned there's room in the business for everybody.

Tony Macaulay had also written the theme music for *New Faces*. He suggested that I should go on it because, apart from the TV time, if you won you were guaranteed 20 weeks' work around all the clubs owned by the Bailey Organisation. I didn't fancy the likes of Tony Hatch and Mickey Most pulling me apart, but I did go along to watch the auditions with him. He was sitting there with Les Cox, who was the producer who decided who went on the show, and a little way back were all the judges sitting with my friend Marti Caine, who hosted it. One act was a wonderful impressionist. His name was David Copperfield. And after his audition he stepped forward and said to Les: 'Mr Cox I'd like to do your show, but for fuck's sake don't let me win because I couldn't stand working for 20 weeks for the Bailey Organisation.' Les Cox loved it, he put him straight on the next show and David went on to star in *Three Of A Kind* with Lenny Henry and Tracey Ullman.

*   *   *   *

Shortly after my first single came out, I was introduced to a Scottish producer called Clarke Tait, a right roughneck. And I paid a stripper £25 to go to bed with him. Consequently he gave me a spot as a singer on a Scottish TV variety show called *Showcall*. Tait used to audition young acts for it, and I was lucky enough to see a folk singer from Glasgow who was stunning. I told him he should come down South with his act, but at the time he wasn't interested. His name? Billy Connolly.

One week we had the great ventriloquist Ray Allen on the bill, with his dummy Lord Charles. I flew back to London with him from Edinburgh and Ray would never allow Lord Charles to travel in the hold; he would take him in the box and strap it onto the seat next to him. As Ray was checking in, the young check-in girl said: 'The other passenger, Lord Charles, where is he?' Ray told her he was in the box. And when she looked baffled he started to have a conversation with the dummy, which was talking back to him. This girl had never heard of Ray Allen and Lord Charles. She was horrified. She was convinced that Ray had put a real person in the box. A half-hour commotion ensued. She called security, and Ray ended up having to open the box up to show her the dummy.

After *Showcall*, I did another Scottish TV production called

Battle Of The Comics which pitted an English comedian against a Scottish comedian and a Welsh and an Irish one. I was the English comedian. Years later we did a 20-minute pilot for ITV with me, Mike Reid, Dave Ismay, John Junkin, Tim Brooke-Taylor, and Barry Cryer. Afterwards, Reid said he couldn't work with me and Dave Ismay, so we all lost it. *Battle Of The Comics* ended up as a show inside a show, with Junkin, Cryer and Tim Brooke-Taylor in the middle of *The Pyramid Game.*

*   *   *   *

A few months after the 1974 series of *The Comedians* ended, Johnny Hamp started *The Wheel Tappers and Shunters Social Club*, which was a variety show with Bernard Manning as the resident comic. Bernard's job was to take the piss out of everyone, which naturally he enjoyed very much. Talking about Gene Pitney he said, 'It's a good job he was nice to me on the way up because I've just met him on the way down.' And when he introduced The Bachelors he said: 'These lads have come a few times now for ten quid and I know full well they can't afford to pay it.'

It was a good show. Liz Dawn from *Coronation Street* got her break on it playing a waitress, and it showcased the likes of Cannon & Ball and Paul Daniels. I didn't appear on screen myself, but Hampy asked me to come along and supply Bernard with what he called 'ideas on material'. I was happy to oblige. I used to go to Manchester and give Bernard and Colin Crompton one-liners.

One week, the late great Tommy Trinder was the top of the bill. I'd worked with Tommy in my early days in the East End, at places like the East Ham Palace and various charity shows. He was a brilliant comedian, fast-talking, and I knew he was a very funny man, always up to date with his humour and as sharp as razor wire. So I said to Bernard, 'Whatever you do – don't take the piss out of Tommy.' 'Yeah,' he said, 'he's all right.' I said, 'No, what I mean is Tommy will take a gag but you have to be very wary of him. He is never happier than when someone heckles him, because that's when he's in his element. He is a very, very clever man.'

But you couldn't tell Bernard anything, he was pig-headed in that respect and my advice was like a red rag to a bull. Bernard decided that he would take on Tommy Trinder and beat him like he'd beaten everyone else. Big mistake.

That night Bernard and Colin Crompton introduced Tommy and he started talking about the old TV game *Beat The Clock* which was part of *Sunday Night At The London Palladium*, because he was the first man to do that long before Bruce Forsyth got anywhere near it. Anyway, the two of them kept trying to take the piss out of Tommy, so he went over to Colin Crompton and he said, 'I'm not saying you don't look well, but don't bother to buy yourself an LP.' And then he went back to Bernard Manning and said, 'That's right, isn't it, Brian?' And you could hear the audience muttering, 'Ooh, he's got his name wrong.' Then Tommy went back to Crompton again and he said, 'I'm not saying you don't look well, but I wouldn't even buy yourself a new shirt, I'd buy yourself a black one if I was you.' And he went back over to Manning and said, 'That's right, isn't it, Brian?'

Well Bernard went in with both feet. He said, 'Excuse me Mr Trinder, you've got it wrong; it's not Brian, it's Bernard.'

'Bernard?' replies Tommy, feigning surprise. 'Oh, I do beg your pardon, I didn't recognise you without a barrel under your chin.'

He had suckered him perfectly and Bernard knew it. So as quick as a flash he just said, 'Bollocks.' And I don't know whether Johnny Hamp couldn't get the scissors in to cut it, or didn't want to get the scissors in, but that exchange was never ever shown.

Anyway, with that, Bernard walked out of the studios and left Tommy to do his act and he was sensational. I learnt a great deal off Tommy Trinder; he might have been blind in one eye but he was one hell of a comedian. He had to keep the Palladium crowd entertained for two hours once during a power cut and after all that, when the filming started, he still had the gumption to say, 'Welcome to Monday Morning at the London Palladium.'

I loved the way he worked an audience. He had one loud-mouthed woman in once and Tommy shut her up by saying, 'Thank your husband for sending you, madam, you must be unbearable at home.' And he had silenced bigger men than Bernard Manning. Orson Welles tried to heckle him at the Embassy Club once. Orson was in a stinking mood because Rita Hayworth had divorced him that morning. Tommy said, 'Trinder's the name', and Orson Welles said, 'Well why don't you change it?' Quick as a flash, Tommy flew back with, 'I don't believe it, he's only been divorced ten hours and he's proposing already.' Orson Welles was lost for words.

King George VI invited Tommy to Windsor Castle shortly after Edward VIII had abdicated. 'Well, Trinder,' said the King. 'You've done well since I last saw you.' Tommy replied: 'You haven't done so bad yourself, sir.' Genius.

Prince Philip copped it too. He'd not long been married to the Queen, and he came along to a Water Rats do at Grosvenor House in the West End. The turns were all told not to drink because Philip would be picking the cabaret act for the evening when he got there. The Prince picked Tommy Trinder, but Trinder said, 'I'm sorry, I can't do it, I'm cruising and I have to go to Southampton to pick up the boat.'

Prince Philip said, 'Mr Trinder, as an old naval man I can assure you that you'll be picking up a ship.'

Tommy shot back: 'I haven't got time to stand here arguing, mate, I've got the boat train to catch.'

It's the 'mate' that gets me.

*   *   *   *

I did do other TV work, but never anything on prime time. After *The Comedians* I pretty much hit a brick wall. I worked behind the scenes – Danny Baker would ask me to come in to *The Six O'Clock Show* on ITV in the '80s. Danny was their roving reporter, and Paul Ross was his researcher at the time. I would go in and give them ideas and gags, like I had done on *Wheeltappers*. They were very funny boys and it was a pleasure to work with them. On screen, however, it was a different story. TV turned its back on me; not because of anything I'd done but because of what the bosses had heard about me. My reputation went before me and according to the word on the street, I was too naughty. They said I was a dirty comic and that I worked with strippers. Well, that last part is true. I did work with strippers and I enjoyed every minute of it. And I am outrageous, but I was never dirty. I never swore on stage. I was barred by people who had never ever seen me work.

I did do some filming for Freddie Starr's *Variety Madhouse* in 1979, but I was cut out of it. It all came about by accident. Norman Collier was taken ill and I was called in to do a warm-up. After that the executive producer at the time, David Bell, called up and said that Freddie wanted me to do the series. I went in on the Monday, found out what the theme for the week was and went away to write material for it. The first week it was The Hunchback of Notre Dame so I did Quasimodo goes to the pub and asks for a whisky. The barman says, 'The Bells all right?' and Quasi says, 'Mind your own business.'

I did eight of them, but before it went out David Bell rang me and said that I'd done very well but I wasn't zany enough and he couldn't fit me in. But seeing as they had Les Dennis on for the next series, which was hosted by Russ Abbot, that excuse didn't really ring true. Les is a lovely bloke but he's about as zany as a coat-hanger.

After seeing the way the show turned out, I was glad not to be on it. Bell did get me in to shoot a pilot with Chas 'n' Dave, but I didn't get the show. They gave it to a comic called Jeff

Stevenson who was one of my support acts. I did once have a conversation with David Bell about why I couldn't get any TV. He said he would give me a late night show at the drop of a hat if he thought it would further my career.

There is a lot of corruption in broadcasting. As well as the Granada executive who'd wanted to get aboard Marion in return for giving me TV exposure, I was approached by the producer of a very famous chat show who suggested that I could be a guest on the show if I agreed to reimburse the host for the £10,000 he'd lost on the horses that week. I wasn't that desperate. I refused and the booking went to another comedian who didn't.

The only TV I did in the '90s were a few late night shows – I was on *Bushell on the Box* on ITV twice in 1996. And other times I was approached it was by shows who were trying to set me up and portray me as a racist, which I am not and never was.

The *Kilroy* show was the worst offender. They booked me for a discussion programme about comedy taboos and they asked me to do the joke about two West Indians walking along the road, and one of them says, 'I've had enough of this country, I'm going home.' His mate said, 'Take no notice of the white trash.' He said, 'The people don't bother me but when the animals take the mickey that's too much.' He said, 'What animals?' He said 'Well last night I was in Trafalgar Square and all the pigeons were going 'Look at the coons, look at the coons...'' – with the last words said like a pigeon cooing. I did it because they asked me to, and some of the audience laughed, but around me it was very quiet because while I was telling the gag, they'd brought in a party of Rastafarians and sat them behind me. And Robert Kilroy-Silk asked them, 'What would happen to him if he told that joke in your club?' And one of them said, 'He'd be lynched.'

But when I turned round and looked at them I realised that they were from the Q Club in Bayswater, which was very racist towards white people (see the chapter Equal Opportunities Offender). The show was pre-recorded and everything I said about this club, which discriminated against white people, was cut from the transmission and it made me look a right idiot. They'd asked me to tell this particular gag to paint me in a bad way and hang me out to dry. I went after Kilroy-Silk but as soon as the show ended he bolted.

I met Paul McCartney a week later at a Nordoff Robbins do and the first thing he said was, 'That Kilroy-Silk set you up last week, didn't he?' I did get my own back eventually with *Kilroy* though. Bill Wyman invited me to a comedy evening at his restaurant, Sticky Fingers. Kilroy-Silk was there with his wife and his daughter and he apologised to me; it wasn't him, he said, it was the producer and the director. Of course it was. It was always somebody else...

Television's attitude to me used to annoy me, especially when I'd see other people on there doing my act. Now I think they did me a favour because the TV ban made me a rich man and a cult.

I think I said that right.

*   *   *   *

Immediately after I left the Montague Arms, I started to work around. I was back in the pub scene, doing The Dun Cow and The Green Man down the Old Kent Road, the Tram Shed at Woolwich and a club in Sidcup, Kent. I was running around everywhere. My reputation had gone before me and I was getting bookings coming in from all over. I was getting offers for weeks of work from as far up as Stoke on Trent and all over the Midlands.

Jollie's night club in Stoke was absolutely fabulous to me. I appeared there with people like Peter Gordeno and Tony Christie. And I met two brilliant acts who again confirmed to me that television wasn't all it was meant to be. Their names were Ronnie Dukes and Ricki Lee. Dukes was a good comedian who did magic tricks, and Ricki was a singing impressionist – her Shirley Bassey take-off was sensational. They were husband and wife. Ronnie and myself sat down after a show and he said, 'They won't put you on telly will they, Jonesy?' I said, No they wouldn't. He told me: 'I'll tell you something Jonesy, count your blessings. The powers that be in television have done you they biggest favour they could ever do you, because the worst day's work I ever did was allowing Johnny Hamp to put me on *The Wheeltappers and Shunters Social Club* because through that bit of telly I lost my act.'

It sounds like a strange thing to have said, but consider this: Ronnie Dukes and Ricky Lee were the best club act in England at that time. They came from Rotherham, they were a family act, very wholesome, very clean, and they had been working seven nights a week, 52 weeks a year. They were in so much demand that they were having trouble getting so much as a long weekend, never mind a holiday, that's how good they were.

But as soon as they appeared on TV with their routine, a hundred other duos started to copy it. They were no longer unique. They had given away their act and got nothing in return for it. That made me think about TV in an entirely different way.

Here is Paul Ross on his memories of working with me:

'Danny Baker introduced me to Jimmy Jones's work and he became a bit of an obsession/guilty pleasure for me. Jones was filthy and funny, like Frank Skinner's lecherous Cockney uncle. He was also old school, proper showbiz – he had the Roller, and was knocking out tapes and albums after the shows, sometimes from the boot.

'Jimmy was too blue for telly and was suspected of being misogynistic/borderline racist and altogether too offensive for TV. In the 1980s I did put up an idea to Alan Boyd – then head of entertainment at LWT and the King of Saturday night – about creating a replacement for *The Comedians*. It was a rip-off of *Joker's Wild* (which was then ripped off by the Beeb as my brother Jonathan's *Gag Tag*.) I called it *North and South* (as in rhyming slang for mouth) and it was to be Northern comics vs Southern ones, with Danny as host and Jimmy and Bernard Manning as team captains.

'In a parallel universe without the (in retrospect) stultifying Saturday/Friday Live alternative comedy mentality, it would have been a zinger; a sort of early version of all those Nine Out Of Ten Cunts shows that are all over the TV now.

'Boyd said he only booked Bernard to add a bit of danger to shows and would stand in the studio staring at him to keep him under control. He knew of Jimmy, and I remember him praising him as a great raconteur comic, but said he could only ever be a guest because of his 'satanic' reputation. Ha!

'Another big Jones fan at the time was Jeff Pope, who is now a BAFTA-winning writer and producer. Jeff became obsessed with the twilight world of the full-on stag show blue comic. He met a young guy who was trying to break into the circuit and had kept a pretty raunchy diary of gags and goings on (girls doing punters on stage, giving comics blow jobs, plus punches being thrown and tyres slashed over nicked gags etc). He wrote it up as a fly on the wall documentary series and spoke to Jimmy for research purposes. He wanted him to voice it as the Grand Old Man of Blue. It was also mooted that Jimmy would mentor this young guy. Jeff put the idea up to Channel Four via Jane Hewland, who was then our head of Features, but no one bit. Another missed opportunity.

'But we did our bit for the Jimmy Jones legend. Danny [Baker] was the roving reporter on *The Six O'Clock Show*. I worked with him and we used to interview Jimmy as a talking head in our silly items. This was the era before proper telly PR, and we suffered because *The Six O'Clock Show* was the first show to transmit in the London region after Thames handed LWT the weekend reins (how clumsy was all that?).

'So in the absence of a proper press office working for us I would slip it out to the *London Evening Standard* and the *Evening News* that Jimmy Jones was on, to drive up the audience. Then one day I finally persuaded the show's then Editor, a lovely man called John Longley who'd worked closely with Boyd on *Game For A Laugh*, to book Jimmy as a live studio guest. Gulp. The item was about the fact that Havering in Essex had no Blue Plaques, and Jimmy came on as a local boy made bad.

'He was a bit sentimental at first about somebody we'd never heard of deserving one for their "charidee" work (even though I'd briefed the silly old sod that you had to be a) dead and b) funny to get a plaque and a mention), but he soon picked up the pace and gave us the saucy Jones twinkle. Then – well, bearing in mind this was around 1983 and a tea time live show – disaster struck. We wanted him to do a gag about Prince Andrew and Fergie getting married, and he started an interminable gag about a fella with a gold nut and bolt through his belly button. There was the floor manager waving, Michael Aspel frantically trying to find an out, me knowing I was in for the mother and father of all bollockings as the show practically crashed off air. And the punch line felt filthy for that time of night, when the belly button was unscrewed by a gnome (!) the bloke's bum fell off or some nonsense. Oh boy.

'I could never persuade them to try him again live, but we did interview him as a talking head for items (I think this is what Jimmy means when he says we worked with him for ideas.) He was a lovely guy, and always very generous with his time.

'Incidentally this is my all-time favourite Jones gag:

'A fella goes into a brothel, he hasn't had any for weeks and he asks to see the price list. This lovely blonde bird behind the counter walks off into the back room and comes back two minutes later with a large board. Written on it are the words: Wank: £10. Blow Job: £20. Straight sex: £40. Backdoor: £50. Cheese Roll: 50p. The fella looks at this bird, and she's really quite special. He says, "Do you do the wanks?" She replies: "Yes, I do." He says, "Well wash your 'kin' hands and get us a cheese roll."

'Classic.'

CHAPTER ELEVEN

MOB-HANDED: VIVA 'KIN' VEGAS

IT WAS MY manager Neil Warnock's idea for me to play Las Vegas. I had no idea I'd end up working for the Mafia.

We flew into Los Angeles first. Neil had got me Raquel Welch's stage manager Matt Leach to run my big debut show. Matt fixed me up with a popular radio show based at the University of California with a famous DJ who called himself 'Lord' Tim Hudson. His claim to fame was he was the first person ever to play a Beatles album in the US. When we arrived there was a bottle of champagne waiting for me, nice and cold, and a bottle of Johnnie Walker Black Label whisky for Neil, so they treated us well, but Lord Tim was a bit up himself. He said he'd never heard of me and so he'd only give me ten minutes at 9pm. A little before he said on air: 'If you want to speak to London comic Jimmy Jones, the lines are open now.' Immediately the phones went ballistic, lighting up this big console like a Christmas tree.

The first caller was Dudley Moore! The second was Tom

Selleck. I didn't finish talking until 2 in the morning. Lord Tim was amazed when Dudley came on. He said, 'What, *the* Dudley Moore?' And Dudley was so good to me, he kept singing my praises and plugging the Vegas show.

A few weeks later when we were all back in England, Dudley came and saw my act at Lakeside at Camberley. He said he'd been working and couldn't get across for the Sahara gig, but he needed his shot of Jimmy Jones sauce. (But the very first time Dudley came to see me it was because he'd recognised me from when I was still called Albert Simmonds – the name my parents gave me – singing 'Ave Marie' as a boy in St Peter's church in Dagenham when he was the organist!) Tom Selleck I'd met when he came over to Kent to film an episode of *Magnum, P.I.* at Leeds Castle. Someone had given him one of my tapes and he'd become a huge fan.

Lord Tim suddenly became a whole lot friendlier!

The calls kept coming, mostly from ex-pats and entertainers. I had a bit of a break after a couple of hours and Neil spoke to callers about Nazareth, the rock group he looked after. Then I came back and rabbited some more. We finally finished by 2am, by which time Neil had demolished the whole bottle of Black Label and no cab company would come and pick us up, so the poor assistant producer had to give us a lift back to the Beverly Wilshire Hotel in her car – and Neil opened her back window and left her a spectacular technicolour yawn all down the side of it.

The next morning Neil's wife took me in to see him. He was comatose on the bed, and she'd crossed his arms on his chest like a corpse. I knew his eyes would open eventually, but it wouldn't be this morning. I had a late breakfast and settled down by the hotel pool with Matt Leach, whose other job was to teach me the differences between our lingo and theirs; things like saying 'sidewalk' for 'pavement', 'trash' for 'garbage', the different meaning of fanny here and there – it's an arsehole to them – and the fact that when a bloke sidles up and asks you if you want to score some shit he isn't trying to flog you a bucket of fresh crap.

It was like going back to school – something I was never much of a fan of. I couldn't say cockerel – they didn't use the word. They called them roosters. And trade names like Biro are meaningless there. If I wanted to talk about a pen I had to call it a Bic or a Paper Mate. Oh, and I had to slow right down so the Septics could understand me. Septic tanks – Yanks. They wouldn't have got that either.

I'd had some experience of this at home, on a much smaller scale. When I first played Manchester I caused some upset in the audience by referring to my wife as a silly cow. I was told that cow was a much stronger word up North than it was down South, where it was an affectionate insult. Years later Chubby Brown called my wife a cunt, which he pronounced 'coont', and was amazed when we got angry about it. According to him, where he came from, Middlesbrough, cunt was a term of endearment while twat was the really bad word. But I think that was just in Chubby's head. I happen to know he was run out of a Northern club once for using the c-word. It was a Catholic club and they'd just been robbed. Roy walked on stage, pointed up at the giant crucifix and said, 'I see you caught the coont who nicked your telly.' Whoosh! That was the end of his set. There was uproar.

*   *   *   *

We flew in to Vegas at night time. It was pitch black. Then the pilot said, 'Ladies and gentlemen, if you look over to your left you'll be able to see Las Vegas,' and there it was, this beautiful, beguiling neon city set in the middle of nowhere.

We were staying at the Sahara, which is now the last of the old Rat Pack hotels at the northern end of the Strip. Stars who have played it include such legends as Sinatra, Dean Martin, Sammy Davis, Judy Garland, Paul Anka and Bill Cosby. The place is steeped in showbusiness history. The promoters had offered me the chance to open for Neil Sedaka in the big room, but I turned that down. I knew that people who came to see Sedaka probably wouldn't come in to see the support act. I could have walked on stage, dropped my strides, bent over and had a flock of doves fly out of my arse and I'd still be playing to a half-empty theatre. Plus there was a good chance my kind of humour would upset some of the more sedate Sedaka fans who did turn up. So I held out to do my own show, and now my name was up in lights in the Mecca of showbiz, 5250 miles from home.

The next day it was my first rehearsal with a trio of musicians. There was a drummer, a bass player and a pianist who was sitting sideways on his piano. I gave them their notes and this pianist started playing the first song in the wrong key.

I pulled him up straight away, saying, 'Listen, I've spent a lot of money getting the sheet music for you, if you can't play the song in the right key tell me and I'll know I'll have to strain.'

An American voice rang out behind me. A man barked at the pianist: 'Do the job properly or you're out.' With that, the man sat round straight away and played in the correct key. He looked terrified. I had three songs in my 40-minute set – 'Wichita Lineman', 'My Way' and Matt Monro's 'Walk Away'.

Afterwards two Americans approached me, including the one who'd bollocked the piano player. They were the Rizzo brothers, my promoters. The other one said, 'Hey, you're a comedian, where did you get that great voice?' I told them I'd started as a singer, they nodded their heads, and on the night of the show I had an eight-piece band.

There was an English fella there I knew, a terrific singer called Alexander Butterfield, and he marked my card about my new friends. 'You know who you're working for don't you?' he said. I didn't know what he meant. 'These are seriously heavy people,' he said. 'You're working for the Mob.' Shit. But now it was too late for me to do anything about it.

I was feeling great about the show, though. I was wearing this fabulous tuxedo from Savile Row. I looked the business. The place was heaving – every Las Vegas entertainer who wasn't working was in the lounge bar to watch me that night. I opened with 'Wichita Lineman' – the band was superb – and I got an immediate standing ovation. The only one still sitting down was Marion. Then I started with the jokes. After a minute or two of going slow, I caught Warnock's eye and mouthed 'Fuck this!' And I went into my normal routine – normal speed, normal words. They got it all right! I ripped 'em apart.

I told them: 'We Englishmen founded this country of yours and we tried to educate you as best we could, but you've changed some of our language. But I am from London, England, and I am going to do this gig as an Englishman and a Londoner and if you don't understand the words, I'll explain them to you.

So I did some stories, and took the piss out of the crowd. There was a group of really beautiful women right at the front. I said, 'Hello girls, what do you do?' And one of them shouted back: 'We're ladies of the night.' I said, 'Well, it's nice to see you sitting up for a while.'

And I did my normal act. They loved the sex jokes. I even did the gag about Noah and his ark:

After the Great Flood, Noah was out on his ark for 30 days and his wife was getting worried. She said to him, the ark's sinking. But Noah said, it can't be, God wouldn't let that happen. So she said, you forgot about the animals' natural functions. And when Noah went down stairs he realised that she was right because there was poop all over the place. So he put his wellies on, got himself a shovel and shovelled this great 'kin' big mountain of poop over the side. And 5000 years later, Christopher Columbus discovered it...

I thought they were going to lynch me, but again I got a standing ovation. Incredibly, I'd stormed the place. It was a dream come true. Yet it had only been a few years before that the great American comic George Carlin was fired by the Frontier Hotel for, in his words, 'saying shit in a town where the big game is called craps'. Times were changing and a dollop of London filth had gone down like a cold pint in a heat wave.

The Rizzo brothers were in to me as soon as I came off stage. They'd loved it. They wanted to pay off Neil Warnock and fuck him off home and take over my career themselves. They wanted me to work the next six months in Vegas at $1500 a week, then six months in Atlantic City for the same money.

It was tempting, but I turned it down. The Rizzo brothers were flabbergasted. They weren't used to people saying no to them. One of them said, 'You do realise we actually run Las Vegas?'

I said I did, but politely explained that I couldn't start with them immediately because I had bookings in England to fulfil. They said, 'Well, don't go back!' I replied that I didn't like to let people down.

They said, 'Well we want you now, get rid of Warnock, we want you lock, stock and barrel.' To smooth out an awkward situation I told them I needed time to think about it. They agreed, but said 'Don't take too long.'

I did think about it, seriously. On one hand it was very tempting. But it would mean taking a drop in my earnings, and also flying out my wife and kids and at the time Grace would not have done it. So it would have meant me being away from my family for a whole year. Neil Warnock thought I should do it. He thought I could break America – a couple of years later Andrew 'Dice' Clay became a stadium act with his brand of shock humour.

I had a long talk with Alexander Butterfield about it, too. He used to live round the corner from me in Dagenham but now he was trapped in Vegas working off his gambling debts, so perhaps his view was jaundiced. But he said to me: 'You like to go to work when it suits you, don't you Jim? Well if you work for the Rizzos you go to work when they tell you.'

We flew off to Hawaii for a couple of days and I made my mind up. Much as I loved the US I'm an Englishman, and I didn't want to live anywhere but England. I told Neil my decision. He said, 'You know if you turn them down you'll never work America again, don't you Jim?' I replied, 'Well, there's enough work in England, isn't there?'

I think I made the right decision.

While we were in Hawaii we were walking down the beach going towards the Hyatt Regency and this voice from behind me shouted out, 'Hello Jonesy, what the fuckin' hell are you doing here?' in a Scouse accent. I turned round and it was George Harrison. I said, 'Never mind me, what are you doing here?' He said, 'John Lennon talked me into buying a pineapple farm down the road, and I can't fuckin' sell it.' George had a fabulous home in 63 acres on Maui's North Shore. We had a drink together and had a pleasant couple of hours. I particularly liked the lyrics to his song 'Taxman' for reasons that will be quite apparent if you remember my problems with the Revenue.

We went back to Vegas for another few days and a couple of comics there were already trying to do my act. Nothing changes.

Marion was badly ill while we were out there, confined to her bed for two days – she was so rough they had to change the sheets with her in the bed. But I did get time to see the sights. I saw Engelbert and Tom Jones's shows and socialised with them. I saw the great American comic Don Rickles do a lunchtime charity show – he was a class act and full of stories about his times with Sinatra. Even driving around was incredible, seeing hotels like Caesar's Palace, The Sands, The Palms and the MGM – legendary places I'd only ever seen in films.

I think if I'd been single I would have stayed and given it a shot. If I'd been a single guy in Vegas I would have been at it like a rabbit. I would have shagged my brains out for six months.

When I got back to England, I told the TV producer Johnny Hamp about my Sahara experience. He seemed very interested in it all, and asked a lot of questions. Not long afterwards I realised why! Hamp took Bernard Manning out to the MGM Grand to shoot a TV documentary for Granada the following November. It went out prime time in February 1978 and made the front cover of the *TV Times* under the headline 'My Great Gamble by Bernard Manning' – as if no English comedian had ever played Vegas before. They cheated too; Bernard did a teatime gig and they gave the tickets away to a lot of elderly Jewish people and had to dress up the crowd reaction with a laugh track.

At least my show had a three-drink minimum!

I asked Bernard for his verdict on it and he said, 'I fucking hated it.'

As well as turning down the Mafia, I also turned down a bunch of crooks who wanted me to play Australia in the 1980s. They wanted me to do two six-week tours for nothing but expenses and then pay me for the third. Bollocks to that. But I have done a week of shows in Cape Town, South Africa, for ex-pats back in 2005, and I very nearly played Germany – see the chapter entitled 'In the Army Now'.

CHAPTER TWELVE

FUNNY WAY TO BE A HERO

IN MY LIFE I've been lucky enough to know and work with some of the real legends of comedy, including two of my favourites, Tommy Cooper and Benny Hill, both heroes to me.

Tommy was wonderful, a naturally funny man – he could make you laugh just by being himself. He was a little eccentric, though. Offstage he seemed nervous and he sweated heavily. He had the biggest feet I'd ever seen – those plates of his were easily size 20. He liked a drink too. He used to say, 'I'll have a gin and water, easy on the water.'

I was at Eastbourne once, playing Kings while Danny La Rue was at the Congress Theatre down the road. Danny was going to come along and watch me, but Tommy turned up at his venue. Well, Danny had borrowed this £5000 sofa from the antiques shop around the corner, which was run by a gay fella who was a fan of his. Tommy dropped himself into it and the whole thing collapsed. Danny was mortified but Tommy just said, 'Sorry about that but it was fucking old!'

Danny had to go and beg the bloke to say that it had happened in his shop so he should claim the insurance.

Tommy couldn't help but be funny, even when he wasn't trying. He was a big clumsy bloke who'd spent seven years in the Horse Guards as 'Trooper Cooper'. He became a comic by accident. He was doing a serious magic act, but he got so nervous at an audition he fluffed the tricks and the agent thought the mistakes were part of the routine, and so the crackpot conjurer was born.

I was up in Manchester with Tommy once when I was doing *The Wheeltappers and Shunters Social Club* and he was doing his own show at Granada. They'd put us in the Piccadilly hotel and asked if we'd mind sharing a cab to the studio. I didn't mind at all, it was an honour and a pleasure to be in his company. Granada paid for the cab but it was customary to give the driver a tip. When we got in the back, Tommy said, 'Leave it to me, Jim, I'll give him a drink.' I thought nothing more of it. Coming back I had the self same cab driver, so I said, 'Tommy looked after you, didn't he?'

'Yeah,' he said. 'He gave me a drink… a fucking tea bag.' Lovely bloke, Tommy, but he was as tight as arseholes.

Bob Monkhouse told me once how Tommy had made him take the tube to the Palladium with him, to save money. Well, this particular day a beggar got into their carriage, a scruffy bastard carrying his dog in his arms. He was quite aggressive and when he reached where Bob was sitting he loomed over him and growled, 'Money for food.' Tommy looked up and growled back, 'Eat the fucking dog,' and then carried on with the conversation.

He did the Royal Variety show one year and when he met the Queen afterwards he asked her: 'Do you like football?'

'Not particularly,' she replied.

'Ah,' said Tommy. 'Can I have your Cup Final tickets then?' Tommy Cooper was a dream to work with, and he was just as naturally funny off-stage as on.

The next time Danny La Rue got upset, I was to blame. It was 1980 and I'd told Grace I was going to Australia to work as a cover story for Marion and myself going for a romantic holiday in Barbados. Everyone around me got told the same thing, the only one who knew where I was really going was my son Steven. Anyway, I was at the Circus Tavern before we went and Danny was the guest act. When Grace told him that I was going to Australia, he sat and wrote a letter to his agent in Sydney which I was supposed to hand deliver. I couldn't tell him anything because Grace was with me. Of course I didn't deliver it and he had the raving hump with me.

When we met up next I bought him two bottles of champagne and a big bunch of flowers to make up for it.

When we got to Barbados we had a whale of a time. I kept bumping into people who knew me, even some poor punter I'd picked on in the Montague Arms. Eddy Grant, who I knew from his time in The Equals, came to the hotel and surprised me. He's a lovely man. Marion and I liked Barbados so much that we sneaked back a year later – only this time I'd told everyone that I was off entertaining the troops in Cyprus. On this second trip I ran into another old friend from London, the train robber Ronnie Biggs. The British authorities had been trying to extradite him from Brazil for years. On this occasion he'd been kidnapped and smuggled to Barbados, but he'd won his appeal against extradition and now he was going back to Rio de Janeiro. There was press everywhere – reporters, cameramen, film crews. I said, 'I'm not being funny Ronnie but can you come and meet us back at my hotel because if I get pictured with you here Grace will have my guts for garters.'

*   *   *   *

I got the train up to Manchester once with Marty Feldman, who was on his way to record *What's My Line?* for the BBC. We really hit it off on the journey. So when I got to Granada and had a phone call in the studio from Georgie Best inviting me to the opening of his new club, Slack Alice's, that night, I got straight on the phone to Marty back in the Piccadilly to invite him along too. Larry Grayson was supposed to be opening the place but he'd gone down with something or someone, so instead as guests of honour they got me, Johnny Hamp and Marty Feldman, standing alongside Georgie for the photos. Marty's bug eyes were really freaking Georgie out. He said to Marty, 'Why don't you look at me when you're talking to me?' Cos Marty had footballer's eyes – one at home, one away. When he stood in front of George, he had one bug eye on me and the other on Hampy. Marty didn't say a word; he just moved down one and stood in front of me so he had his eye on Georgie. I can't put into words how funny that was. All the press men were in hysterics. I socialised quite a bit with Johnny Hamp. He was nearly a Cockney boy himself – he came from Carshalton and I'd worked pubs there, and we found that we had a lot of mutual friends. He liked a bird as well. After that false start, we got on very well.

*   *   *   *

It was wonderful meeting comedians you admire and discovering that they were lovely people. The late great Benny Hill used to come and watch me every time I played Southampton. He'd sit up in the gods, helping himself to the cleaner jokes. He was quite open about it once when he came backstage before a show I was doing at the Circus Tavern and said, 'Jimmy, if you see my hand moving under the table I'm not having a J Arthur, I'm only nicking the jokes.'

He never tried to disguise it. He liked to steal my gags and turn them into sketches for his TV show, or adapt them to use as lines in his songs. He stole some of my dancers too. Louise English danced for me before she became a Hill's Angel, and I put a dance group together for my Jimmy Jones Show in Eastbourne called The Lovers who defected to Benny in their entirety. Before they were famous, Pan's People danced with me. I'd always wanted to be in Pan's People – one at a time.

Benny Hill wasn't a big swordsman, his 'kink' if you like was oral sex. All he wanted from a girlfriend was what he called 'lip service'. Benny once showed me round the flat he had over near Regents Park. The *TV Times* had just given one of the rooms a make-over, and they'd put green carpet everywhere – on the floor, on the walls, and even on the ceiling. He looked up and rolled his eyes. 'How the heck am I supposed to Hoover that,' he said.

Benny Hill was a big, big fan of my act. He was convinced that television was nearly ready for me, and that he had paved the way for me to have my own show. He said, 'It's proven that people want to see what you do because you're working to full houses.' He set up meetings for me and everything but it was never to be.

Through Benny's friendship I met Michael Jackson, but not until after Benny had died. Some of my kids wanted to see Jacko at Wembley and I pulled a few strings to get them 12 seats. Then the message came back, 'You will be coming yourself, won't you? Michael wants to meet you.' Well, I felt obliged to go after that, and so before the show I was summoned to the Dorchester to meet him. He had the whole of the seventh floor and there were so many security men about you would have thought the UN were meeting. Shaking Michael Jackson's hand was like grabbing a lump of wet fish, but he was a nice enough fella and easy to talk to. He told me that Benny had told him all about me and that he had bought Jimmy Jones videos and noticed that some of my jokes had ended up in Benny's shows. 'It's a pleasure to meet you, Mr Jones,' he said. 'Any friend of Benny Hill's is a friend of mine. Enjoy the show and thank you very much for coming to see me.'

At the show we were given VIP seating. I'd never been much of a fan, but when I watched the man work it was stunning. His charisma, his choreography, his performance was breathtaking.

The press said Michael Jackson was mad, but he was a

beacon of sanity compared to Freddie Starr. What a weird one he is. Freddie was obsessed with Elvis Presley. He always used to ask Tom Jones what drugs Elvis had been on; he wanted to do the same drugs as Elvis. He wanted to die like Elvis. When he did his *Audience With...* for ITV, he even had Presley's backing singers, The Jordanaires, flown in for the show so he could sing with them. But having said that, when he was on form, Freddie Starr was sensational.

The funniest person I ever knew was Spike Milligan. But one of the nicest people in the business was Billy Dainty, the comedian and dancer. He did a summer season down in Torquay and on the opening night he took a bow at the end of his act and his syrup fell off – his syrup of figs, his wig. Very calmly, Bill bent down, picked it up and dusted it off, and said, 'Oh well, you might as well know the lot.' Then he took out his three false teeth. It absolutely stopped the show.

*   *   *   *

I got to meet Long John Baldry when I was working a lot in Manchester. He was a big fucker, six foot seven and as gay as a day out camping in a pink tent with Dale Winton. He was a sensational blues singer and he'd had a massive hit with a song called 'Let The Heartaches Begin' which had got to No 1 in 1967. Anyway, he was staying up in Manchester appearing at the Talk Of The North at Eccles and the Broadway at Oldham, because that's what you did in those days, and rather than stay in digs one of his friends had offered him the use of his house for a fortnight on condition that he looked after his Dalmatian.

So John agreed, he came up early and met the dog and settled in for his two weeks of house-sitting. He'd only been there for two days when the dog got out and was run over and killed. John was in a panic. He phoned Georgie Webb, my manager at time, in hysterics. Georgie calmed him down and said, 'John, it's a Dalmatian and all Dalmatians look alike. Go out and get him another one.' Well, lucky enough there was a lady in the area who bred them, so John was able to go along and buy a Dalmatian the exact same size as the dead one. For the next ten days when he wasn't working John stayed in that house with the dog and when he did go out he made damn sure all the doors and windows were locked. After his final Saturday night show, Long John came back, fed the dog, patted its head and left the key behind, and shot off back home to London.

On the Sunday afternoon John phoned the guy to ask if everything was all right.

'No, it bloody isn't,' he snapped.

'What do you mean?' asked John, trying to keep a note of panic out of his voice. 'What's wrong?'

'It's the dog,' he said. 'I've had to get rid of it. I've only been away for a fortnight and when I got back in the house he never recognised me. The bloody thing bit me!'

From that day to this, the poor sod doesn't know that it wasn't his dog.

*   *   *   *

Shortly after appearing on *The Comedians*, I was working down in Grays in Essex, where I was the compère of the show.

FUNNY WAY TO BE A HERO

I had to do the first half and then another comic did the second. It was what they called a double. When I got there I was surprised to see the top of the bill sitting in the dressing room. It was Roy Hudd.

'You're here early,' I said.

'No,' he replied. 'I'm here on time because I want to watch you, I've already heard that you're a very good comic and I don't want to do anything that you've done.'

I told him that I wouldn't be doing anything that he did but he said he wanted to make sure. Roy was already a TV name at that time, he had his own TV show and had just started the *News Huddlines* on the radio. He had a great love of Max Miller and the music hall and we became instant friends. We're still friends today. Roy is a clever man and a cracking comic actor.

One of the greatest comedians I ever worked with was Bob Monkhouse, a gentleman and a real master craftsman of comedy, very bright and an extremely good gag-writer. I first saw Bob work when I was 17; I was appearing at the Comedy Theatre but I sneaked in to Raymond's Revue Bar in Soho to watch him. Even then he was terrific. He had a lightning quick mind, and a prodigious memory. He could produce a joke on any subject at the drop of a hat. His timing was impeccable. I also saw him appearing at The Windmill, London's famous bare-chest revue, with quite a lot of comics.

I had the honour of appearing with him at the Walthamstow Royal Standard, and because Bob was on I didn't do any comedy. I just sang and the only trouble was Bob hadn't needed a band so the only musicians I had to work with was a pianist and a trumpeter, which meant I had to be very careful what songs I picked out because there's not much you can do with a trumpeter and a pianist.

Years later, in the summer of 1972, I was doing quite a lot of Sunday concerts and an old booker at London Management, Charlie Munyard, sent me to do a show at the Winter Gardens at Margate where Monkhouse was top of the bill. Bob had total recall and he never forgot anybody. I remember that I sang 'My Way' in my slot and I was surprised when I introduced Bob Monkhouse that he came out and sang 'My Way' too. But then when I listened to the words he had rewritten them and made the entire song about me and strippers and my blue reputation. I wish I could recall the lyrics because it was very funny. You can imagine the interpretation he put on lines like 'I ate it up and spit it out' and 'the record shows, Jim took the blows'. He was such a clever man.

Afterwards I had a good chat in the dressing room with him because Bob always made time for everybody. His advice was simple but made sense, if you're a comedian don't cause problems, go to work, do your job and get out. And that's exactly what I am all about, I go to work, I don't create problems. I let everybody else do their job – the lighting man, the sound guy etc – and I ask them different bits and pieces, but I don't tell them what their job is. Treat people with respect. Bob was a lovely, lovely talented man, and he was right. Everything he said was true.

A decade or so later, Bob got in touch and he got me booked for his BBC1 bingo game show *Bob's Full House* two or three times, which was rather nice. He insisted on opening the show with jokes, Bob would always shoe-horn what he called 'funny putty' into every show he did. And because he was older than me, he always referred to me as an up-and-coming comedian, which was nice. He was a wonderful comedian.

CHAPTER THIRTEEN
ALL THAT JAZZ

AS SOON AS I started to get a reputation at the Montague Arms as an act who could pull in punters, I had a lot of people wanting to manage me. Most of them were unscrupulous or at best on the shady side, and of course they all promised me the earth if I let them look after me. A fella called Maurice King came down to Peckham and said he wanted to be my manager for 25 per cent of everything I made, which was very kind of him. Then another man showed up called Don Frost, who also wanted to be my manager; and I thought, what's exactly involved in this management lark that they wanted to do? Most of it seemed to involve taking a quarter of my earnings for doing fuck all but they all painted a wonderful picture of what they could do for me. Don Frost told me he was David Frost's brother, the lying bastard, and promised me he'd get me on TV. He told me he'd got me a night at Caesar's Palace, in Luton, and that they were paying £75. Well I said, 'I'll definitely have that!' because at that particular time I was getting £150 a week at the Montague.

When I got to the club, I met the boss George Savva who asked me all the usual questions, did I swear, what was 'kinnell' all about and so on. It was a Sunday night and he turned to me and said, 'Right, young man, this is the first night of Jimmy Jones week.' Hang on a minute. Jimmy Jones *week*? I was only booked for one night. That dozy bastard Don Frost had booked me in for a week for £75! I told Savva straight: 'You're 'aving a fucking laugh, ain't you? £75 for a week, I'm earning £150 in a pub, why do I want to come here?'

'Oh,' he said 'It's the prestige. This is a top class night club not a South London pub.'

I said: 'Do you know what? My bank manager doesn't take prestige cheques, he like cheques with money on them.'

Savva said that I would never work at the Caesar's Palace again. I shrugged and said, 'Well that's your choice.'

He puffed himself up and said, 'You've got to learn, to get on in this business you've got to do prestige venues like this.'

'No, Mr Savva, I have to go to work for money mate. Do you go to work for money?'

'Yes.'

'Well so do I and if you ain't paying me the right type of wage then I don't want to work here.'

And that was it. I did the one Sunday night, never got paid, I walked out back to the Montague and Don Frost went out of the window like a rocket.

Years later, however, my stint on *The Comedians* lifted me

up a notch. All of a sudden Jimmy Jones became a name that meant something. Out of the blue Caesar's Palace were back on to me and now they wanted me as top of the bill, which was lovely, and that £75 a week which I had originally been offered turned into £500 a week, and that's when I knew that I had arrived.

*   *   *   *

In 1976 I did a charity show in Dagenham for guide dogs for the blind. There was an American act on the show, a blind singer called José Feliciano who'd had a huge hit with a cover of The Doors' song 'Light My Fire'. We got on very well – he was a funny bloke, he once said, 'I was going to dedicate this song to Jackie Kennedy but I can't see her anywhere in the audience.'

José was managed by Cyril Wayne and after watching me Cyril asked if he could manage me too. He stayed with me for nine months and nothing much happened. He started to talk to Bob Wheatley about me doing the Circus Tavern. I had a show there, I was a tremendous success and Bob wanted to offer me a summer season. I asked him to sort it out with Cyril, but he blew it all by asking for too much and that was the end of our relationship.

But I'd managed to open the doors to the Circus Tavern and shortly afterwards Bob asked me to compère the show which had Tommy Cooper top of the bill. On the night, I introduced the great man and we heard this voice say, 'I'll be with you in a minute, I'm just washing me hair.' We all thought it was a joke, but Tommy really was washing his hair, so I had to go back out and sing another three songs before we could get him on stage.

Tommy was lovely, but he liked a drink. We all went back to his dressing room beforehand and he said, 'Hello Jim, what do you want to drink?' I replied a lager, and he said, 'Good idea, I'll have one with you.' Then Grace asked for a vodka and tonic. 'Good idea,' he said. 'I'll have one with you.' Whatever anyone asked for, Tommy would drink as well. It was fatal, and that's why promoters used to stop people going backstage to see him until after the show.

At the Tavern, he sat there drinking with people so late that when we left he said, 'Ain't that a lovely moon?' And his driver had to tell him it wasn't the moon, it was the sunrise. I did a gig at the Golden Garter at Wythenshaw; I got there for a band call at 5pm and there was a commotion in the corner. It was the staff carrying out Tommy Cooper from the night before.

*   *   *   *

After I'd told Don Frost to jog on, I came to realise that I would need proper representation if I wanted to get on in the business and the man I went with was someone who I'd known for a long time. His name was Georgie Webb, a respected jazz musician; he was as straight as a die and I would have trusted him with my life.

Georgie was a self-taught pianist out of Camberwell in South London. His old man had been in the music halls but Georgie's passion was always trad jazz. He got into the business when he worked assembling machine guns in the

Vickers-Armstrong factory in Crayford, Kent. He put on jazz concerts at the factory, and founded his own band the Dixielanders to play the music of 1920s New Orleans. His heroes were people like Louis Armstrong and King Oliver, and at the time I knew him in the '70s, Georgie was looking after such people as Acker Bilk, Kenny Ball, Bob Wallis – all the trad jazz greats.

Georgie got me good jobs for good pay. One was a lunchtime gig with Acker Bilk in the West End. Afterwards Acker invited me back to his club in Dean Street for an afternoon drink. Now licensing laws were very strict then, and at 4.30pm the police raided the club for after hours drinking. Six cops came in and they had to ask us what drinks we had so they could keep a record of what the club was serving. Acker Bilk was as pissed as a parrot. This copper said to him, 'Excuse me Mr Bilk, what are you drinking?' Acker replied, 'That's very decent of you, I'll have a large gin and tonic.'

*   *   *   *

Naturally, with George Webb as my manager, I was introduced to the world of jazz. One day he invited me up the 100 Club in Oxford Street to see a certain famous American jazz trumpeter.

This Yank was coming in to do two shows in London and then he was flying on to West Germany to do a massive jazz festival there. He was a very impressive looking guy, handsome, tall, black. A big, big man. He must have weighed about 27 stone. And he played like a dream. Fabulous he was.

Well, there was a fella in the audience, another Yank, who absolutely idolised him and he insisted on holding a reception for him after the show. The fella was loaded, and he threw this lavish do back in his house at the Quadrangle at Marble Arch.

The big jazz star went on stage at 10pm and finished about midnight, whereupon all of us made our separate ways to this rich American's house. His wife was very house proud, and the gaff itself was like a film set, with wonderful ornaments and amazing white carpet. You didn't Hoover that carpet, you raked it, that's how beautiful it was. But of course by then the trumpeter was hammered. He'd been on the whisky and rye all evening and he was standing in the hall, still drinking, when he leant on this lovely antique writing bureau which collapsed under his weight. The bureau had two ink wells in it, one black and one red; they smashed and the red and black ink went all over this white carpet. Understandably the poor wife started screaming her head off. So Georgie hustled the jazz star out and that was the end of the night.

Of course, when he came to the following day at midday, he had ink all over his hands which, naturally, puzzled him. I was there with Georgie and we told him exactly what had happened. The poor fella was mortified. He said, 'Well I've got to apologise to this lady, get me some flowers and we'll go round and say sorry to her.' One of the band popped out and got a lovely bunch of flowers and we all went back to Marble Arch. By now, mercifully, the wife had calmed down but her carpet was absolutely ruined. The red and black ink hadn't just splattered the hallway; it had got onto the carpet in the lounge as well.

ALL THAT JAZZ

The lady very graciously accepted the trumpet player's apology and the flowers, she could see he was cut up about it, and she asked him if he'd like a drink.

He said, 'Yes, please, ma'am, whisky rye.'

'Well, sit yourself down,' she said. And he dropped himself in an antique chair in the lounge. But as he sat down the legs of the chair buckled and it was smashed to pieces. Once again, the wife started screaming like crazy. The big jazz star raised an eyebrow. 'Ma'am,' he said. 'It's only a chair. I'll buy you a new one.'

'No,' she replied. 'My dog was sitting underneath it!' The poor little dog had been killed outright. He had broken his back, so once again we had to get the big fella out of this house as quickly as possible.

I told a version of that story on stage once but, in my reworking of it, the jazz star asked to use the khazi before he went. He came out saying, 'That's a mighty fine gold toilet you have there, man.' To which the rich Yank replied, 'You silly bastard, you've just shit in the French horn!'

Georgie Webb opened some very nice doors for me. I was never the top of the bill for him, I was always the support act, but he got me some very good support. Georgie only died in March 2010. He was 92, and known as 'the father of British traditional jazz'. Several members of his band went on to be well-known. The clarinetist Wally Fawkes became better known as the cartoonist Trog. The trombonist Ed Harvey was a founder member of John Dankworth's Seven, and the young Humphrey Lyttelton got his start as Georgie's second cornetist. From the 1950s on, Georgie concentrated more on running his agency and was doing well until 1973 when he sank most of his dough into promoting a jazz festival on the Isle of Man. The building burnt down in August of that year, soon before the festival was due to begin, and Georgie lost most of his investment.

*   *   *   *

After I parted company with the Montague I had a day or two of worry. I was used to a resident job and earning regular money, what was I going to do now? But almost immediately the phone started ringing and agents like Jack Sharpe and John Lyons, who worked for London Management, were putting work my way. I went everywhere. Anywhere that wanted me I would play. I started to do some of the northern clubs again; there was no chance of the work drying up.

Jack Sharpe had an agency down here called North Come South. Jack started to put a lot of shows together with Jimmy Jones as top of the bill, and we were literally all over the south of England. He coupled me up with good Northern acts that didn't mean a thing down here in the South, they were great turns but they didn't mean a light here. One time he said he had a great girl impressionist singer from Sheffield and asked if he could put her on the show with me. Her name was Lynne Stringer, but you will know her better by her stage name of Marti Caine. She was wonderful, a funny girl who did great voices, and we became very good friends while she was down here in the south. Some of the Northern acts we brought down would repay the favour and take me back up North to support them.

John Lyons played a rotten trick on me once, though. He and Jimmy Smith gave me a job one night in Great Yarmouth when I was still singing as well as doing the comedy. But when I got to Yarmouth, the band demanded £5 a man to play for me.

'Forget it,' I said. 'I'll do an hour of comedy.'

'Really?' one of them replied. 'I suggest you go and have a look at the audience before you make that decision.'

I walked out there, and the place was full up with Mormons. There was a woman actually sitting in the front row feeding a baby on her tit. So I said to the boys, 'You've got your money', and I didn't do any comedy at all.

I phoned up Jimmy Smith the next day and I said, 'You're a bastard doing that to me.' He laughed and said, 'We just wanted you to sing, Jim.' What a dirty bastard, what a thing to do to an act.

*   *   *   *

A guy came along to see my show, and afterwards he came up and said, 'I want you to do my club in Norwich.' I said, 'I don't normally work anywhere where they still point at planes.'

I thought Norfolk people were too busy shagging their relatives to come out to clubs. But they did. And that's how I started a residency at the Talk Of East Anglia. It was a great club for me. I worked there Thursdays, Fridays and Saturdays, but to keep food on the table I had to work the other nights too, and for quite a while I found myself doing Birmingham for the other half of the week with Alan Millican and Tom Nesbitt, better known as the vocal duo Millican & Nesbitt.

They were former miners from Northumberland and they had won *Opportunity Knocks* more weeks on the trot than any other act in the show's history. Hughie Green loved them and he had them back for the show's grand finale in 1978. We worked some very strange clubs indeed, and some of the guesthouses and bed and breakfasts were like something out of *The League Of Gentlemen*. We stayed in one place called Hampton-in-Arden in Solihull, West Midlands, a place I'm amazed the *Carry On* writers missed. It was an odd B&B, for starters you had to make your own breakfast. I was with them for six weeks and we had many long conversations but their accents were so thick the only words I ever understood when they said them were 'Newcastle Brown'.

At the time, their agent was Len Tucker – the guy who got me in the recording studios the first time.

When I finished in the Talk Of East Anglia on a Saturday night, I would get up and drive back to London to work Sunday dinner times in various pubs. I was also doing stag shows with comics and strippers for a fella called Benny Palmer. I learnt a lesson there as well, because Benny made me be the pay master; it was my job to weigh out all the different acts. One particular occasion I was compèring a stag at the Elm Park Hotel. Mike Reid was top of the bill and there was another fella on the show, a good comic called Tommy Dean. But I made a big mistake with Tommy. He slid up to me and asked if I could pay him before he went on stage because he said he had to shoot for a train from Elm Park Station, just next door, as soon as he came off.

ALL THAT JAZZ

So like a fool I gave him his envelope that Benny Palmer had given me and went on stage to introduce him. And I'm gesturing and saying, 'Put your hands together for Tommy Dean', and no Tommy Dean appeared. He'd been paid and he'd pissed off! So I had no choice but to go on and do his 20-minute slot before the stripper came back to show the crowd a slot of her own.

As it happens Benny Palmer got his own back because after that he never booked Tommy Dean again.

I ended up getting a plaque from the Talk Of East Anglia because they worked out that over five years I had entertained more than a quarter of a million people. And that's some going.

One particular night I was getting ready to go on stage and I was standing by the bar psyching myself up when a gas bottle fell on me foot. It hurt like buggery but as soon as I went on stage the adrenaline kicked in and I forgot all about it. When I came off stage, however, the natural high of performing wore off and the pain kicked in again. I was in agony with this poor squashed toe but by then it was 2am. I went back to the hotel and this toe was getting bigger and bigger; the pain by now was absolutely unbelievable.

Marion was with me at the time and she said insisted on taking me to hospital, Norwich General. This doctor had a good look and said, 'Oh yes, I can see what you've done there, lay on the bed.' Well I watched him and he was undoing a paper clip. I thought, 'What the bleedin' hell is he going to do with that?' He put this paper clip over a Bunsen burner and held it there until it was red hot – I mean the thing was glowing – and then he got hold of my toe and poked this red-hot paper clip through the nail and into my toe.

Well, apart from fainting and shitting myself, the blood hit the ceiling. It went straight up like a geyser! But the pain went straight away. I finished up with a bad toe for about a fortnight. I couldn't wear a shoe or anything tight for the next four nights, and finished up going on stage in a 'kin' great boot. Which got laughs in itself, because I had to become the first sit-down comic. Mickey Pugh, a very good London comic, introduced me, the curtains opened and there I was sitting on the stage apologising to the audience for the obvious big 'kin' boot. I quite liked having to wear it because it meant that for seven or eight weeks I could nick all my shoes from outside shoe shops.

I love it when birds shag me in boots. It's 'kin' great. The people who work there get a bit pissed off about it though.

*   *   *   *

During my time at The Talk Of East Anglia, I got to know some of the directors of Norwich Football Club. I love football and used to go and watch the Canaries at every home game. Johnny Bond was the manager, we became good friends and he and most of the players used to come and watch my show on a Saturday night. One particular Friday, he offered to fly me up to Manchester for the match and get me back in time for the evening's show. I jumped at the chance, and ended up on the plane with one of the sponsors, a gentleman by the name of Sir

Arthur South, a furrier. This pleased Marion because she loved furs and she had fur coats coming out of her ear holes.

On the way up, Sir Arthur said, 'Now, we're in Manchester United's Directors Box, you will behave yourself Jonesy won't you? No bad language.' I assured him I didn't use bad language, just 'kinnell'. So we get there, we get in the lift up to the box, me, Sir Arthur and Ray Alders, one of the Norwich directors, and as the doors open for us to get out who should be standing the other side but Sir Matt Busby. He took one look at me, and his words were, 'Hello Jonesy, what are you doing up here in 'kin' Manchester? Don't expect me to sign you, I've got enough comedians in this team.' Sir Arthur's face was a picture.

Bill Shankly was the funniest manager I ever met; he had a story about everyone. It was Bill who came out with the classic line: 'Some people think football is a matter of life and death; I can assure you it's a lot more serious than that.' I went to Liverpool once for one of Bill's team talks. He told Tommy Smith that he was marking Georgie Best and he wanted him to put him out of the game. Tommy said, 'What happens if I break his leg and get sent off boss?' Bill Shankly replied, 'Don't worry son, they'll miss Best a lot more than we'll miss you.'

*　　*　　*　　*

During my time with Georgie Webb, the agent John Lyons booked me for Jollees Cabaret Club at Longton, Stoke-on-Trent, which was the largest cabaret venue in England at the time. I got there on the Sunday afternoon, and the manager, a fella called Mike Massey, was very off with me. 'What are you doing here?' he said. 'I cancelled you this morning.'

I stood my ground and I said, 'Nobody has told me that you'd cancelled me. I'm here and I have a contract here to say that I'm booked for the week.'

He said, 'Well I'm telling you now, you mention one swear word on that stage and you're out of here like a fucking shot.'

'Hold on, hold on,' I said, 'What are you talking about?'

He said, 'You're a blue comedian', so I said very firmly that I wasn't and once again I explained the kinnell catchphrase. So he let the show go on but he still insisted that he would be watching my act like a hawk. As it happens, it was a very good bill. Peter Gordeno was the headline act, and he was a wonderful dancer. I tell you, this guy must have taught St Vitus. People remember Peter now more for being in the sci-fi series *UFO* but he had redefined entertainment dance on television introducing a very fluid jazz style of dancing.

After the first show, I came off and Mike Massey came straight backstage shaking my hand and apologising. 'You were fabulous,' he said. I thanked him, and then I asked what had prompted his panic earlier. He explained that on the previous night, the Saturday night, he'd had a couple of people in, one of them a comedian himself, and that they had told him that I was a very blue stag comedian and that if he let me appear it would mean his club would be closed. I asked him who had told him this, but he refused to say. But I was angry now, I explained that if someone in the business was going around telling lies about me I needed to find out who because obviously this could be very damaging. But Massey wouldn't say who it was.

So I decided to turn into Miss Marple and have a sniff around. The sound engineer was a lot more forthcoming, and I'm sad to say the identity of the lying bastard will not come as a great surprise. It was Mike Reid.

Reid had been on the bill and he and another guy, who turned out to be Lena Martell's musical director, had gone out of their way to blacken my name. The sound man told me that they had gone around telling everyone who would listen that Jimmy Jones was a dirty comic who would eff and blind. Once again Reid was my nemesis. But he was never as clever as he thought he was, because Mike Massey made up for the misunderstanding by booking me for Jollees more times than any other comedian. I did the club with Ronnie Dukes and Ricki Lee four times in the next year, and three times with Tony Christie. And they always treated me well and looked after me. Only once did I have the tiniest of problems there. I'd been booked on a week when Mike Massey wasn't there and he'd told me on the phone, 'Behave yourself this week Jonesy, because the top of the bill is a bit worried about you.'

The top of the bill was Roy Castle, he was on TV a lot and was renowned as an all-rounder: singer, dancer, comedian, trumpet player; a jack-of-all-trades. Mike wasn't there for the first two nights but on the third day he turned up at the near-by pub where I was staying. He wasn't happy. 'Jonesy,' he said, 'what have you done to me? You've let me down. Roy Castle has complained. He reckons that you are too strong for him.' I told him that I was doing nothing out of the ordinary, just doing the same act he'd seen me do before; a few different gags and in a different order maybe but nothing he wouldn't have been expecting. I was mystified and I think Mike was convinced that I was telling the truth. He shook my hand and went off but half an hour later he came back and apologised.

He said, 'Jim, I've got to say sorry to you yet again, but there will have to be some changes. I've just read my manager's report about the top of the bill and unless he changes his act by tonight, you're changing places with him, and he will be your support. The reason he wanted you off the bill was that you were going down better than he was.'

CHAPTER FOURTEEN
DEAD MAN DRINKING

Fella goes into a bar and orders three large whiskies. He looks as white as a sheet. And as soon as the barman serves him he knocks back these whiskies and orders three more. As he downs the sixth one he says to the barman, 'I shouldn't be doing this with what I've got.' The barman says, 'Why, what have you got?' The fella says, '76p.'

IN 1976 I ended up running a pub by accident. At 5am one Sunday morning I had a phone call from the police. They'd found a dead body outside the pub door. I naturally replied, 'It's nothing to do with me officer, I don't serve spirits after time.'

What had happened was a couple of local herberts had dug up a corpse and left it propped up outside the boozer. My wife Grace was horrified. She said, what, there's a stiff 'un on the doorstep? I said, 'I've got a stiff 'un here, get back into bed.' But the cops took it a bit more seriously.

My pub venture began by chance when my wife asked me if

I'd finance her brother John, who wanted be a publican. I got him to go and see what pubs were up for sale and, in a very short while, he came back and said there was a lovely pub in Enfield called The Kings Arms, known locally as the Top House. I got him to spend a bit of time there, have a drink, count the customers and see what the clientele was like. Less than a week later he came back raving about the place. He thought it was perfect, so I set up a meeting with Ind Coope, the brewery involved, who were very interested in Jimmy Jones having a pub. Ind Coope gave me a nine-year lease, which was unheard of at the time: normally you only ever had a five-year lease. And that was it, I got the pub.

It was situated in Enfield Highway, and it was frequented by a lot of travellers, who had a camp at the bottom of Green Street. The place was a shit-hole, to be truthful. It was more of a tip than a top house. There was an old sofa upstairs, which stank, so we threw it out the window into a skip and when it landed I watched two dozen mice run out of it. They had been living in the sofa.

We did the whole place up, made it look the business, and re-opened it. Within eight weeks my brother-in-law decided that he didn't want to work the pub anymore, he'd gone overnight, so now I was lumbered with a boozer and a nine-year lease. I had to run the place myself while I tried to find a manager. I put one of my daughters in, Helen, who was actually underage but she was a good barmaid, and I was perhaps a little too hasty in employing a couple called Terry and Gill to run the pub. I started to put on entertainment, too, discos to start with, and then I brought in some radio DJs – Tony Blackburn, Dave Lee Travis and my good pal, the soul DJ Robbie Vincent – I'd known him a couple of years because from about 1974 I used to go on his BBC Radio London show straight after the Montague Arms and do a comedy hour between 11 and 12pm. People used to phone in jokes and I'd vet them and stop them if they were going to be blue.

As well as the jokes we used to get a great deal of messages to read out and what we didn't realize at the time was that certain of these were aimed at the boys in prison so that particular part of the show was stopped by the management, but we had a good time.

Robbie could only do one Sunday a fortnight for me, so I used to do the other Sunday mornings and Sunday nights myself and we took a hell of a lot of dough. That was when we earned our money. We were bringing in guest artists, Robbie brought in the Real Thing, Denise Williams, Clem Curtis and The Foundations, who'd had a big hit with 'Baby, Now That I've Found You'… and he brought in all the record producers who were doing promotions. The Kings Arms became the place to be.

I turned an upstairs room into a gymnasium and had some of the unlicensed boxers train there – Donny 'The Bull' Adams and Roy Shaw. I wasn't really into the boxing scene but I made a few bob from it, and the fighters were never a problem. The people who gave me the most grief to start with were the manager and manageress. They were a nightmare.

For some unknown reason Gill was never there when I got

to the pub on a Sunday evening. I used to turn up at 7.30 and the place would be full up and I had to serve behind the bar myself because there was no Gill. I didn't mind working behind the bar, I used to enjoy it, but I had get from there to on stage and introduce Robbie Vincent and the guest artists, which was never easy.

On other Sundays I had a DJ called Tony 'Shades' Valance who was a far better jock than Robbie Vincent, but because Robbie was on Radio London he was a bigger name and a bigger draw.

So I gave Gill a pull about her not being there to open up, and she said that she always used to go and visit her sick mother on a Sunday, which made her late. I'm a big softie so I swallowed the story, until one of the fellas said to me unless her sick mum lived in the Top Rank bingo hall in Enfield, Gill was telling porkies. He said he'd been playing bingo with her since 5pm.

I decided to catch her out, and also to check out how much she was spending, because I had my suspicions that all was not right with the pub finances. In those days a manager and manageress's wages were £65 a week 'cos they got their accommodation slung in for free, and I let them have the food takings as well. So I paid this fella to follow Gill on the following Sunday, and sure enough she was at bingo from 5pm until 7.30.

He sat behind her and clocked her spending £110 because she played the one-armed bandits as well. £110! This could explain a lot, I thought. I paid the guy to follow her for the next couple of Sundays as well. Gill did exactly the same both days except the spending went up; one week she lost £120, the next £130. I had a stock take and by sheer coincidence I was down £250 on the stock. So on the Monday I sat them down and I sacked them. Terry just shrugged and said that he was glad to be out of the pub. All of the clientele were arseholes, he said, especially the Wild Bunch who came in at the weekend. Wild Bunch? I had no idea who he was talking about, because even though I'd been running the pub I was still going out and gigging most nights.

I decided to take the next Friday and Saturday nights off and, just as he said, this so-called Wild Bunch got in there and they *were* arseholes. One of them shit in an ice bucket and put it back on the bar. Another one bit the head off of a chicken and let it run around the bar. They were bastards. I went absolutely ballistic at them. But one of the cocky gits turned round and said to me, 'This is our pub, and you can't do nothing about it Jonesy.' I thought, we'll see about that.

As you know, earlier in my life I'd worked for some villains, who were always nice people to me. One of them was a man I am going to refer to just as Johnny Brixton, 'cos he spent a lot of time giving Her Majesty pleasure in Brixton prison. He was a very famous villain but he wouldn't appreciate me telling you his actual name.

I got in touch, took him to lunch and told him the problem, and he came up with a plan. The following Sunday I invited the Wild Bunch to stay behind for a lock-in after the lunchtime session had finished, and you could see them thinking, yeah, we've won, we've got Jonesy under our thumb now. All eight of them stayed behind, and I poured them a pint of lager each. Then I said, 'Now, you've caused a great deal of problems in this pub. You've broken windows. You've frightened people. You've dragged blokes outside and beaten them up. You're not people who I want in my pub.' Then I introduced them to my friend, Johnny Brixton. And when they saw him, they shit themselves. I said, 'Mr Brixton is here in a friendly capacity today but if I have to ask him back in a working capacity I wanted him to see the people he'd be looking for.'

These eight fellas went white. Johnny turned to them and said, 'I know each and every one of you. You all think you're big boys. You don't know what big boys are. If Jimmy sends for me in a working capacity, even if he mentions just one of your names, I'll be looking for all eight of you.'

And after that, I didn't have one ounce of trouble from any of them for a long time. They were the Mild Bunch from that day on.

With the problem sorted, I gave the bar management job to a good publican called Nobby Clark. His wife, Smokey, an ex-stripper who I'd worked with, was pregnant so they wanted to move out of South London.

I still had eight years of the nine-year lease to run, and I couldn't sell it because, although we were a good music pub, we had quite a few fights in there so it had a got a name as a trouble spot.

It wasn't long before Nobby disappointed me too. I soon noticed that the bar takings were down and that the pool table and the juke box weren't taking as much money as they used to.

When I mentioned it, Nobby shrugged and said it was just swings and roundabouts of the pub game. I wanted to believe him because I trusted him, but I still decided to check things out. I had a week off but I told Nobby I was going off to have a residency in a club in Leicester. On the Monday, I came back to the pub. It was deserted. There was no Nobby and no Smokey. There was just a young girl behind the jump (working the bar) who I didn't know, and who didn't know me. I watched her pull her boyfriend a pint and not take any money. That's nice, I thought. On the Tuesday it was the same story. No Nobby, no Smokey, no punters, and this bird giving my beer away; Wednesday, the same. On the Thursday we had a group in and so Nobby finally appeared. It was busy so he never saw me, and on the Sunday I asked him how the week had been. He told me Monday to Wednesday had been a bit slow.

I said, 'I'm surprised you know,' and then I told him that I'd come in every night and that I knew exactly how little work he'd been doing.

'I can't work for a bloke who spies on me,' he said, faking indignity.

'Good,' I said. 'That will save me sacking you.' Nobby and Smokey packed their bags and went.

So now it was back to square one. I had to somehow run this pub while I was also doing shows all over the country. The solution was to put my girlfriend Marion behind the bar with my daughter Helen and my wife. I had my son Peter, who was 12, changing the barrels in the cellar. We all used to sleep in the pub as well. It was a real family affair.

Which is when the incident with the dead body occurred. The police took it very seriously and they told Grace that they wouldn't let us open up. But Sunday mornings were best for bar takings, so out I went to try and change their minds. This one copper was there standing guard over the mummified body, which he had covered up with crates and empty cardboard boxes from the pub. Not much dignity in that – going out like a bag of cheese and onion crisps. He pulled back the boxes back to show me the corpse, which still had hair on the skull. Its mouth was wide open. I said, 'Well, it's gotta be a woman.'

That got a laugh. I asked him why they hadn't moved it, but they were waiting for a pathologist to make sure it was dead. I said, 'Are you having a laugh? It's mummified. That's as dead as George Roper's nudger.' The copper said it was procedure. Luckily the pathologist turned up and by 11.45 they'd taken the body away – 14 minutes before opening time. The cops asked me to try and find out where it had come from, but what amazed me was that they didn't want to know who had done it: digging up a corpse was classed as body-snatching and if they found out the culprits they would have got put in prison for five years. Which was a bit much for a sick practical joke.

That night I went on stage and said, 'One of yous lot has had a joke with Jonesy. Well done. Now I don't want to know who did it, you think it's all a big laugh, but you could end up doing a five stretch for this, so someone had better tell me where the body was dug up so the Old Bill can put it back in the consecrated ground it had come from.'

Of course, by then the national press had got hold of the story and it made the papers. And for days we had busybodies and ghouls turning up from all over to see if the body was still there; but by then it was in the morgue at Shoreditch.

Six months later I received a note saying that the corpse had come out of Highgate Cemetery, the fourth tomb along from Karl Marx's grave. It turned out that the body was 180 years old.

Inevitably it had been a present from the Wild Bunch. One of them in particular thought he was going to have a laugh at my expense. He'd stood it up against the door hoping that as I opened up in the morning the corpse would have fallen on top of me. But a friend of mine called Bert had been passing the pub at 4am and thought it was a dummy! So he got out of his car and moved it, and he still had no idea it was a real dead body.

Another problem arose while I was away with the family on holiday. Marion was running the pub, and the Wild Bunch, although they were still on their best behaviour, were persuading Marion to have lock-ins until 4am. I got back from holiday and got called in by the police who had the names of everyone who'd been having afters. I had to knock that straight on the head or I would have lost my licence.

Soon after that a regular called Les asked for a drink one Saturday lunchtime after time. When Marion told him we would no longer be selling drinks after time, the nasty bastard grabbed her by the hair, pulled her behind the bar, wrapped the phone cord round her neck and said, 'I will murder you unless you give me another drink.' She refused him again and he smashed the phone and walked out. Marion rang me, she was in pieces. I was at home in Hornchurch and I shot straight over, it was the fastest I've ever driven – Hornchurch to Enfield in 25 minutes. Now, I'm not a fighting man but I wasn't going to stand for that. I told this Les's mates that he was barred from the pub and said, 'Tell him I wanna see him, I'll meet him in the car park tomorrow.' The following lunchtime he turned up after the show. He looked white. He was drugged up to his eyeballs, he stank of Pernod and he had an iron bar behind his back. Typical coward. He'd hit a woman, but with a man he needed a tool.

I said, 'You can hit me with that iron bar if you like but if you do make sure I don't get up because I have got enough money to have you put in a box and for no one to ever find you.'

He dropped the bar and said, 'Can I come back in the pub?'

I said, no, you are banned for life. He drove down the road, got pulled up by the police and got done for drunk driving – nothing to do with me, just a nice case of what goes around comes around.

Around this time I took on another manager, Cyril Wayne who was also looking after José Feliciano and a great soul group called Clem Curtis and the Foundations. I was telling Cyril about my problems with the pub and he put Clem behind the jump for me. Clem was from Trinidad, and he'd been a pro boxer so he was a handy fella to have in a pub. I was doing a great deal of black material at the time, with the voices, and Clem loved it.

Shortly afterwards I got a tip from someone who worked

for the VAT people that they were investigating me and they were going to raid my pub. Of course, I'd already had the problem with the Inland Revenue and I didn't need any more grief. So I found some publicans who wanted to buy it, the Collins brothers, and then I had to talk the area manager into allowing it because there was still five years left on my lease. In the end I had to give him a backhander to let the deal go through, a nice drink it was too.

I got out of the pub in May 1980, paid off all the bills and wound up the company I was trading as. Two weeks later, the VAT inspectors raided the place to find a new owner – Bert Collins.

Irish fella playing poker with his mates in the pub, loses all his wages on a hand, has a heart attack and dies. One of his pals calls his wife. He says, 'Your Paddy has just lost all his wages playing poker.' 'Oh, has he,' she replies. 'Well tell the 'kin' bastard to drop dead.'

*   *   *   *

I fell in love with the island of Menorca after spending a week's holiday there; and in 1976 I bought a holiday villa in Cala En Porter for £9700 – paid for at £3000 a month for three months out of the pub takings. We'd stayed at a villa that belonged to a Canadian musician called Gib Wallace, who used to be one of the top trombonists in England. The poor sod had had a motor bike accident and smashed his face up and after that he never blew a trombone again.

We decided we wanted to buy our own place out there and Gib knew that the fella who lived opposite him was selling his, so the two of us became neighbours. What a character this guy was. One day he came over to my villa at 7.30 in the morning and Grace asked if he'd like a drink. He said that's fucking decent of you. So she said would you like tea or coffee. He said, 'I haven't come over here to be insulted. I'll have a gin and lemon.'

The silly sod had gone out in his car the night before and couldn't remember where he'd left it, so he wanted me to drive him about looking for it. We went all over the south of the island searching for this poxy car; four hours we were gone, and we eventually found it outside a bar 500 yards from where we lived – it had been there all night with his dog in it.

A few weeks later, Grace woke me up at 4am because there was a car in the middle of the road with its lights on and its engine running. I went out to investigate and it was Gib's car, but there was no one in it. His door was open so I went to see if he was OK. I called out and there was no reply, so I went in and saw Gib lying on the bed with a local guy called Domingo, and there seemed to be blood all over their shirts. This frightened the bloody life out of me. I shook him and Gib came to. I said, 'Where's all this blood come from?' But it wasn't blood at all. He'd made them both tomato soup and where they were so pissed he had spilt it over both of them.

The worst thing I've ever seen involved a musician in Menorca. I won't say his name because he is still alive and it's hugely embarrassing. He'd gone into Mahon and pulled a

With soul singer Deniece Williams –
she was very partial to my Pina Colada.

Inset: A Jones Christmas card.

'It's Christmas,.... I'm pregnant.... God knows how,....
and you tell me you forgot to book a room,
....'Kin ell' !

Above: Meet the family! The Jones clan turned out in force for my 50th.

Below: Training with Frank Bruno in the Peacock gym in Canning Town – I let him win.

A charity night at the Elm Park hotel, with ex-barmaid Nora as the world's least
likely bunny girl.

Above: On tour with Dave Lee and impressionist George Marshall down in Torquay.

Below: On stage at Jollees Cabaret Club in Longton, Stoke.

Left: With my granddaughter Lisa.

Right: Live at the Talk of East Anglia

Above: Appearing on *The Wheeltappers and Shunters Social Club*. © *Rex Features*

Below: My charity soccer match at Rainham Football Club.

Above: At Lakeside having won the *Club Mirror* Comedian of the Year award.

Below: Backstage at Lakeside with Mike Reid, Linda Nolan and funny girl Ellie Laine. Mike Reid had to present the *Club Mirror* award to me – and he hated every minute.

Above: Presenting a charity cheque during the darts tournament at the Tavern.

Below: With my personalised number plate, K1NEL; it could have been worse, it could have been KN0B 0UT.

young German lady who'd invited him back to her place. When they got there she tied his arms to the head board and his feet to the bottom of the bed. She stripped off his trousers and pants, he already had the horn, and then she told him: 'I think all men are pigs.' He said, 'Yeah? Well all women are shag bags.' And with that she produced one of those big 'kin' safety pins like the kind you see on kilts, and drove it straight into his nuts, right through his nut sack, and clipped it shut. Then she left. This musician was in agony. He created enough noise for someone to come and rescue him. He got a cab back to Cala En Porter and one of the locals, Miguel, got him pissed on brandy and then he came and got me. We applied ice cold water to his bollocks to take the swelling down, and Miguel kept on feeding him booze until he passed out. Then we were finally able to pull the pin out.

The next problem was he was due to fly home to England to meet his wife on the Monday – I had to ring her up and say he'd missed the plane. All week I had to come up with different excuses for him not coming home while he waited for his bollocks to heal up.

This woman wants a piercing but she wants something a little bit different so she gets a diamond stud put in her Jack and Danny. Posh twat. I caught me tongue in it and panicked. I was in a right old flap.

CHAPTER FIFTEEN

WIZARDS AND WARNOCK

'When I first saw Jimmy Jones on stage he looked like a redundant pirate. He wore shirts with ruffles, over-sized collars and big balloon sleeves. He could have been in Pirates of Penzance. *I said to him, "Jim, where's yer buccaneers?" Quick as a flash he replied "Under me buccan-hat."* – Neil Warnock

IN 1976 I was contacted by a gentleman called Neil Warnock, the MD of the prestigious rock agency Bron. He now runs The Agency, which is massive worldwide. A record promoter called Roger Bolton had played him my tapes and Neil wanted to come and see me live. I invited him down to Kings on Canvey Island where I was working a hen party, and not thinking too much about it I invited him along to see it. The place was heaving with women and their hands were everywhere. Neil Warnock had never seen anything like it. The poor sod got covered in bruises just walking backstage with me. His arse was black and blue. They touched him up too. It was a little bit different from the Nazareth rock audiences he was used to. The stripper had a chopper like the proverbial baby's arm holding an apple. Neil didn't know where to look.

I don't really like playing hen shows because it's mayhem so I only did a 15 minute slot. It was pointless trying to do comedy to them so I just sang. I did Tom Jones, Engelbert – all the hip thrusting stuff they liked. Warnock must have enjoyed it because he insisted on coming along to my next proper show, which was at the Circus Tavern, and he saw the whole hour-long act. Afterwards he said he had laughed for the whole hour and there and then he offered to manage me. All he wanted was ten per cent. It was a gentleman's agreement, no contracts, just a handshake. Neil said he could have me playing theatre tours and make me a TV star. Well, he did get me theatres. He got me Vegas and the Palladium too, but telly work always eluded me.

At the time I was on the ropes because of the taxman clobbering me, so the prospect of lots of decent, well-paid work appealed.

My act was already out on video: I was the first comedian to put blue comedy on video. And that taught me a lot. I learnt things. I learnt about continuity, I learnt if you're filming two shows to turn into one video, make sure you wear the same 'kin' suit.

I filmed *Live At Kings* so long ago that the first version was actually released on Betamax. Since then it has come out on

VHS and DVD as well. I pioneered the entire adult comedy market! I'm to blame! Mike Reid used to say to me, 'You'll never get on while you're blue'... then they all followed me. I went on to record and release *Newmarket Classic* in 1987 and then *As It Happened* followed by *The Best of Jimmy Jones*, which took classic material from shows at Eastbourne and The Golden Garter, Manchester and *As It Happened* and mixed it together with some unseen gems.

But what Neil Warnock did was to take the comedy video game to another level. At the end of the 1980s, he got me the first ever multiple VHS deal with PolyGram for three new videos over four years. That sort of deal had never been done before. All of the videos went gold, all of them were big sellers. The first time I got a gold disc, Warnock got Linda Nolan to walk on stage and present it. It was a lovely moment and it took me completely by surprise.

The level of sales made PolyGram hungry for more. My videos did so well for them they came and asked me if I could recommend any other adult comedians. Back then Jim Davidson wouldn't go blue, but I told them to sign up Chubby Brown and Bernard Manning. They asked me to call Bernard about it and his first words were, 'How much?'

They'd never heard of Chubby. I gave them George Forster's number and they signed them both. The rest was history. All of the other comedians followed suit: Jim Davidson, Mike Reid, Jethro (who had been very clean up until then). They all jumped on the adult video bandwagon. Yes, folks, I am to blame.

So all these clean comedians who were on TV were suddenly doing videos and effing and blinding and yet the TV people still wouldn't let me have so much as a late night show.

It was the video company who advised me to drop 'Kinnell' and go with fuck. I thought, well they must know the market, so I went bluer. I must admit, I was struggling a bit for material by the time we'd recorded the second of the three videos. They ate up a lot of gags. By the time I got to record the third of the new ones, *Harder and Faster* at the Becks Theatre, Hayes, I had brought in Mickey Pugh as a writer, and he's very good – I must remember to pay him one day. I came on stage in a pearly waistcoat with two bikini-clad blondes pushing on a market man's barrow full of fruit. This was good because it was different. It looked colourful. It meant I could tell the women in the front row, 'Come on luv, if you can grab 'em you can have 'em!' And what no one in the audience knew was that I had simple prompt words written on all the apples and oranges so I wouldn't forget the new material I was doing!

Yes I know what you're thinking, wouldn't it have been easier to have used an autocue. And yes it would have been, if I didn't struggle so much with reading.

The blondes nicked my cucumber too, and I think they had their eyes on the marrow.

I told the audience about the man who developed an apple that tasted like fanny. He let his mate have a bite and he said, 'Urgh, that tastes like shit.' The fella said, 'Turn it round.'

I did give 'em some lovely stories and I also explained the

mystery of why women get crows' feet around their eyes, leaning forward, squinting and saying: 'You want me to suck what?'

*   *   *   *

The late '80s were really a second golden era for me. I'd made my name at the Montague Arms, but at the Circus Tavern in Purfleet I was playing to 1100 people a night. I had a good team around me, and I was even making the news.

In 1988 some poor bloke died laughing in the audience at the Tavern. He'd had a fatal heart attack – the doctors said his heart had been beating between 300 and 500 times a minute. He was only in his 50s. I was pretty shaken about it as you can imagine, but his family thanked me. They said he was a big fan of mine, and that they were pleased that he'd died happy. The story made *The Sun* newspaper, but it didn't end there. His son was a jeweller and he came and saw me a few months later and thrust a present into my hand. He had taken his dad's jewellery and made it into a ring for me with JJ on it, made from gold with diamonds on the Js. The son said, 'Dad would have loved you to have this.' What a lovely gesture. I've treasured that ring to this day.

I was the king of the Circus during the 1980s. I held the record for bar-takings with my audience there, only the darts crowd drank more. That record held until the West Ham-loving rock band the Cockney Rejects played there a couple of years ago.

Now Neil Warnock was looking after all of my bookings,

and he put my wages up. He was asking for £3000 a night – and we got it. Neil opened a lot of doors for me. He got me in to the Bailey Organisation and to places like Bailey's at Watford, Blazer's at Windsor, and the Lakeside Country Club at Frimley Green, the best cabaret room in Britain at the time. The boss at Lakeside, Bob Potter, didn't want to have me there because he'd heard that I was filthy. Neil Warnock just said ask the Circus Tavern how much they take on beer and grub when Jimmy Jones is on. So Potter was intrigued enough to try me, I banged the place out for him, and after that he was booking me for weeks at a time.

One of Bob Potter's rules was he didn't allow the acts out in the audience. He had an artists' bar backstage and once I got to know him we got on ever so well.

That first week Frankie Vaughan came in to see me and asked if I minded him recording 'Loving You Ain't Easy', which was nice of him. Frankie nominated me to be a Water Rat, but I was blackballed. Although not as badly as the poor sod in Menorca with the safety pin through his nuts.

Once Bob Potter became a friend he proved to be very loyal. There was a royal show at the club in a week that I was booked to do, but the organisers didn't want me on the bill. Bob insisted that I was his act for the week and if they didn't want me they could poke their royal show. Which is how I came to be on the same bill as Gloria Gaynor. We had a pre-show reception, and Prince Philip came straight over to me. 'Hello Jim,' he said. 'Nice to see you.' I introduced him to Neil Warnock and Gloria Gaynor – 'And what do you do?' he said to Gloria. He had a gin and tonic, but not until after we'd had some pictures done because he wasn't allowed to be photographed with alcohol. He asked what time I was going on, and when I replied 10.15 he said, 'Shame. I'll be gone by then. As soon as they give me the cheque I'm buggering off. Have you got a new video out?'

I did indeed and I made sure he got four copies.

Gloria Gaynor was devastated that he left early. She'd flown in specially for the show, and Prince Philip didn't even get to see her.

*   *   *   *

I did three more of my vinyl records from the Tavern, all on my own Kinnell label. And we did three different pantos there, including a *Cinderella*, with an emphasis on the sin – yes, Jim Davidson nick-nicked that idea from me too! The Tavern loved having me because when the crowd got a bit lairy, when there were stag and hen parties in for example, I could always handle it because I'd honed my act in rough pubs.

My problem was Christmas time; I was in so much demand I often did two shows during the day, sometimes three, as well as the Tavern in the evening. The problem wasn't the work, I loved to work. The problem was there were times when I couldn't remember if I'd done a gag already in the set I was just doing or in the one I'd done a few hours before.

*   *   *   *

I was still signed to Neil Warnock, who also had other top-flight rock bands like The Stranglers, Simple Minds, OMD, Pink Floyd and Status Quo. Through Neil I got to present Status Quo with a gold album in Paris and I got to meet Pink Floyd in Geneva. We had a wander round the stadium and when we went backstage again we found Marion being served bangers and mash by someone she called 'a nice chap': David Gilmour, the band's guitarist. David loved Marion because she had no idea who he was and talked to him like a normal person. Gilmour doesn't like to be recognised. He's into it for the music, not the fame.

Warnock also got me involved with the Nordoff-Robbins musical therapy foundation, with a lot of the rock stars. Quo were involved, Paul McCartney, all of Iron Maiden, Dave Dee. We raised a lot of money. One of my favourite fund-raising venues was School Dinners restaurant in the West End, where all the waitresses dressed as schoolgirls, and the male staff dressed like Eton boys. Rick Parfitt seemed partial to a caning from one of those schoolgirls, I can tell you. I did one show a year there for five years and over that period we raised half a million pounds for Nordoff-Robbins.

In return they gave me a very nice award.

Another rock star I was surprised to work with was Lemmy from Motörhead. What a lunatic he was! Nice fella, though. That was in the late '80s. It was a big charity event, organised by June Brown from *EastEnders*. I hosted the show. Lemmy came on and played on his own with a guitar. I sat and talked to him afterwards and he told me about his wild days with Hawkwind when the group did lots of LSD. He told me,

'They'd get high in the park and talk to trees and sometimes the trees would win the fucking argument.' Crazy bastard.

*   *   *   *

Warnock booked me in to Bournemouth for long summer seasons – we did ten-week runs for three summers, which was very enjoyable. I had a lot of music in the show, and Jimmy Tamley the ventriloquist; it was a real comedy variety show and we built up to very good houses. That variety mixture worked at the seaside but the music didn't go so well on the road.

Away from the Tavern, I carried on working my way around the country, generally in the South. Neil put me into theatres that no one else in the business was doing. Other comics said we'd catch a cold but I was getting good houses, selling out the Beck at Hayes and theatres in Yarmouth, Stevenage, Southampton, Northampton, Devon, Cornwall.

Usually when I toured, Warnock would put on a musical support. He'd have Linda Nolan or Rose-Marie opening up for me. Linda's skirts were so short she used to get a lot of fellas in on the off chance they'd see her draws. But Rose-Marie wore longer skirts and so I'd find there were always more people in the bars than there were watching her. The arrangement wasn't working so I started to use a comedian as a support instead: I used Mickey Zany for the first run, and I had a band with me. Then Dave Lee became my first regular warm-up comic, a very funny 18-stone former drummer from Kent who lit up the stage with his smile. His comedy was gentle and he didn't swear so he was a good contrast to me – plus I knew that he wasn't going to nick my material. One night I was working at the Dartford Orchard and Dave and Crisco, the comedy magician, both stripped off and chased Crisco's missus who was also stark naked across the back of the stage. This went down so well that Dave carried on doing it when we were on tour together, but he always timed it between gags so I didn't lose a joke.

After about three years Dave wanted a bit more so I gave him to Jim Davidson as a support. He's still with Jim to this day.

In 1988, after Dave, I began using Mickey Pugh, a very good Cockney comic who would grab hold of the audience with three or four quick-fire gags and then once he got their attention he would do 40 minutes of observational comedy about real life, work, school-days and growing up poor. His 'two drunks' routine is legendary on the circuit – and still to this day he's up the pub every night fine tuning it. In many ways he was and is London's answer to Peter Kay, but he was doing it first. Mick and I were light and shade. He'd go out and be squeaky clean and talk about life, and then I'd come out and do Kinnell.

One of the funniest ever nights with Michael was when I was mistakenly booked to do the Wembley WI. Mick was looking at the letter thinking this must mean Wembley Working Man's Institute, but it wasn't, it was the Women's Institute – the same mob who did for Tony Blair! It was mistaken identity: they thought they'd booked Jack Jones. We got there and the audience was 300 women all sitting in rows.

Mick went out first and warmed them up with his lovely clean nostalgic routine, and then said, 'Ladies, please put your hands together for the legendary Jimmy Jones.' And 300 women said, 'Jimmy?'

I went out and said, 'Well there's obviously been some sort of f...f...mess up here. I'm one of those rude comedians, but I'll try and keep it from slipping out. Madam, you'll let me know if it slips out won't you?' Nothing. So I went on, 'If I feel the need to swear out of respect to you I will say the word cabbage instead and you can guess what I meant to say. OK. This woman had this lovely big pair of 'kin' cabbages...' Whoosh, they were gone. I pulled the place apart.

Another time down in Torquay, I'd booked us all into a bed and breakfast run by a couple of gay guys. But Marion didn't want to stop in a B&B, so I booked the five star hotel round the corner for us, and left Mick in the B&B. We did the show, came back for a nightcap with Michael, and then left him drinking in the bar with some travelling salesmen until 4am. I'm not a big drinker but it has to be said that very few people can keep up with Mickey. He's even built his own bar at the end of his garden which he calls Arkwright's.

We had to drive to Rugby the next day, and when I arrrived to pick up Mick he was still dead to the world. So I asked one of the staff to wake him up. This fella looked like Lurch from *The Addams Family*, and he was dressed like Lurch, too. He went up and shook Mick who came to and found a strange man in his room, grabbed him by the throat and slammed him into the other bed. I heard the commotion and ran up to find

Mick strangling this poor hotel guy. 'Mick,' I said. 'Put him down, that's your early morning call.'

*　　*　　*　　*

It was Neil's idea for me to play Blackpool. I only did it once, once was enough. What a shithole that is. I was on at the South Pier, and I met the compère. He told me he was a singer, and I said good, I don't want you doing any comedy and I don't want to hear you swear. Well, when I got back there from the hotel he was on. I could hear all this effing and blinding and outrageous jokes. His spot lasted for 20 minutes. So when he came off stage I pulled him up.

'Oi,' I said. 'I thought you said you didn't do gags.'

'I don't,' he said with a look of wounded innocence. 'That wasn't me, I was miming to one of Chubby Brown's tapes.'

'You were what?'

'I was miming to one of Chubby's comedy tapes.'

I think he called himself Chubby Arse, or he might just have been a chubby arse. The next night I saw the real Chubby on the North Pier, told him about what had gone on, and by the next morning the Chubby imitator was out on his arse. Chubby's management had him taken off the pier.

I didn't enjoy Blackpool, and even though I was offered more work there, it wasn't for me.

Much worse than Blackpool, however, was my first Butlin's show. Neil got me on an adult weekend at the Pwllheli camp. I did the Friday and Saturday night, Bernard was doing the Sunday lunchtime. When I got there the band asked me how long I was going to do. I replied about 45 minutes. They said, 'Billy Pearce only managed 12.'

The audience were ferocious, but I was doing OK. It was a full house. I was 35 minutes in when there was a big cheer. This young girl walked on stage, she was about 20 stone and she was shouting out top of her voice, 'So you're the fucking guv'nor, are you... you taught Chubby fucking Brown.' I had a brief pointless discussion with her but she wasn't taking much in. I asked if she was from Manchester. She said, 'No, I'm from fucking Newcastle.'

I said well Bernard Manning is here on Sunday and he would love to have a chat with you. Make sure you go and see him.

Then she said, at the top of her voice: 'I'd liked to fuck you.'

'Well listen darling,' I replied, 'I'd like to fuck you, too, but I'm afraid your twat will be as big as your mouth. Thank you and good night.'

The next night the place was heaving and everyone is waiting to see if this fat bird is going to come on again. Twenty-five minutes into my act, I start doing my Indian restaurant routine. And I'm having a laugh with an Asian boy in the front, saying, 'Don't you do big crisps?' when this fella from Liverpool shouts: 'So you're a fuckin' racist.'

I said, 'I'm talking about an Indian restaurant, so I'm using an Indian accent; it's an impression. I'm not a fuckin' racist, and neither am I one of those people who have to come to Butlins for his holiday. Good night.' And I walked off.

The next morning I rang Warnock and Neil went mad at

Butlins for not giving me any security. I got an official apology from the company and I must have done all right there, cos I still do Butlins now.

*   *   *   *

During the time I was with Neil, I realised I was starting to get a bit Mutt and Jeff. I think it was a consequence of all the times I'd worked with bands in noisy pubs. So I've worn a hearing aid for about 15 years. I woke up a few months ago and found it in bits. One of the dogs had chewed it up. Two grand that cost to replace.

> A deaf couple get married and find that they have trouble communicating in bed in the dark. So the wife comes up with a solution. She says, 'At night, if you want sex, reach over and squeeze my left tit one time. If you don't want sex, reach over and squeeze my right tit one time.' He says: 'Great idea. And if you want sex, reach over and pull my nudger once. If you don't want sex, reach over and pull it 97 times.'

Warnock phoned me one day with a surprise. The great Barry Humphries had taken time off and I had the opportunity to replace Dame Edna at the Aldwych Theatre. I would have my own West End show for five nights. Lovely. Me in the fuckin' West End! You couldn't believe it, could you? But now I had to work on a special West End show. I got a band together, I got a Robin Reliant which I lowered on to the stage, and I got a hat stand with six hats on it; each hat represented a routine. There was a copper's helmet, a bowler hat, a top hat, an army hat, and a Rastafarian woolly hat. I would ask the audience which hat I should do next, and it was always the Rasta hat they wanted.

Simon Porter, who is now Status Quo's manager, was doing my press and he got me *The Six O'Clock Show* with Michael Aspel. I went in and spoke to Danny Baker and Paul Ross and they told me to do a gag about the fella with the gold nut and bolt in his belly button which is mentioned elsewhere in this book. Aspel cut me short and there was a furore afterwards. Why had I done this joke gag? I told them that Danny and Paul had asked me to do it! The producer wasn't happy but I didn't hear of any complaints from the public. From my point of view doing the telly was a great success because it put a lot of bums on seats. We had 98 per cent business all week! That's nigh on a full house for five nights on the trot. And Richard Wilson came along as well. Yes, Victor Meldrew. At the reception, he said, 'I couldn't do what you do. If it's not written down in a script I couldn't say it.' All together: I don't beee-lieeeve it.

*   *   *   *

Sadly my time with Neil Warnock came to an end in the early 1990s. It was all over a tape, an audio cassette, that I was knocking out and which Jackie Thomas had manufactured. The tape was basically the sound track of one of my old videos.

Out of the blue I got a phone call from Neil. He said, 'I hear you've done a tape with Jackie Thomas, why wasn't I involved?'

I explained that it was an old show, but he wasn't having any of it. He said, 'Me and you are finished from today.' And we were, which was a shame; but as far as I was concerned I wasn't doing anything wrong.

Neil Warnock has a different take on it and, in the spirit of fair play and because we go back a long way, I'm going to let him have his say too: 'Jimmy comes from a different time, he's part of that old school East End mentality of them and us, with them being the tax man, the Old Bill, the council – authority really. So he was always trying to nick a bit of extra dough on the side. On one hand he was a very shrewd operator but on the other hand he was quite naive; he thought he could get away with things.

'I'd introduced Jimmy to a producer called Jackie Thomas, who then produced some of the videos we made and some years later she went direct to Jim about another project, an audio cassette, which he accepted a deal on without talking to me about it and without even telling me he'd done it. So he was selling this tape at his shows behind my back, which for me was the final straw. I felt that he had done the dirty on me. From my point of view I'd taken him from Canvey Island to the London Palladium, and from the Circus Tavern, Purfleet, to the Sahara Hotel in Las Vegas, and I deserved to be treated better than this. We were friends as well, we used to socialise together and go on holiday together, which made it all so much worse, although it was probably a mistake on my part to have made a friend of a client. I felt let down.

'I'd been frustrated with him anyway because Jim didn't take my advice on a lot of things – he wouldn't pay for new material, he wouldn't play Australia or devote any time to cracking the US. To be honest I think I'd taken him as far as he could go, and we both knew it. It was a great shame. Because in his day, Jimmy Jones was the guv'nor and there was no one to touch him.'

CHAPTER SIXTEEN

IN THE ARMY NOW

THE FIRST TIME I entertained the troops was in Northern Ireland, in the early 1970s when the troubles were really kicking off. I certainly pick my moments. The army took our safety very seriously. I had a couple of plain clothes men to look after me – I called them Bodie and Doyle – and they changed the car we used daily for added security.

The bill was me, a comedy magician called Crisco and a three-piece band; and they stuck us in a bed and board somewhere down by the border. It was run by a fella who could have walked straight out of *Father Ted*. He greeted me by saying, 'You've got the top room, sir, 'cos you're top of the bill.' I had a shower cabinet in the room, but it wasn't connected to the mains, so there was no water and the room was freezing. I turned the heating on and went downstairs and while I was gone the Irish fella must have come in and turned it off again. I switched the heater back on and Crisco called me. I popped in to his room for a minute or two and blow me when I got back the heater was off again. I went downstairs and confronted him. I said, 'Either you've got big mice or someone's turning off my heater.' He said, 'You can't be having the heater on if you're not in the room, sur.' I said, 'It's cold!' He said, 'Get in the bed, sur.' Cheeky bastard.

I got up early in the morning and nipped down to the shops to buy a copy of *The Sun*. Bodie and Doyle went ballistic. They said, 'You can't go wandering down the shops on your own, someone will shoot you.' 'Why would anyone want to shoot me?' I asked. They replied, 'Because of your English accent. Every time you open your mouth it's an invitation to be shot.' That brought home to me how dangerous it all was. I thought, Christ do I need this? As it happened the gigs were great, except that most of the squaddies were Northerners and I'm not a Northern act.

I went and entertained the troops in Germany too, and I wasn't too happy about that either because they made troops who'd been on duty all day come to the show and told them, 'You will clap.' And I had to go on at 2am the next morning when they were all pissed.

Jim Davidson asked me to go back again in the 1980s and I agreed but when I spoke to the organisers I told them I had two conditions: I wanted a hotel outside of the barracks, and I wanted it in writing that if they booked me to play a Friday, I would play the Friday and not at 2am on a Saturday morning. They agreed and they flew me out.

I got to the barracks and the major told me, 'Here's where you're staying in the sergeant's quarters.' I protested that I was supposed to have a hotel, and he said, 'No, you're in here.' So already I wasn't happy, and so I thought, right-o, I'd better clear up everything else then.

'I'm due on at 11pm,' I said.

He snapped back: 'You will go on when we have finished eating. You haven't got a snowball's chance in hell of going on at 11pm, we won't finish serving the food before midnight.'

'OK, my friend, please tell me, does it state on my contract that I am booked for Friday?'

'Yes it does.'

'Well, after midnight it is no longer Friday, it's Saturday.'

The major just glared at me.

'You are in the army now,' he barked. 'So you will do what you are told.'

Bollocks to that. I picked up my bag, walked to the front gate, got a cab to the airport, changed my ticket and went home.

I never heard from the army again.

CHAPTER SEVENTEEN

YOU, ME, 'IM

ONE OF THE earliest comedy tapes I recorded was called *You, Me, 'im*, which I recorded at King's club on Canvey Island. In the early '80s I got myself a personalised plate to match: U ME 1M. I'd driven all over England in it, but I ended up getting stopped for it by a copper in Upper Rainham Road, Hornchurch, not far from where I lived. This constable asked me to get out of the car, while his mate measured the front plate with a tape measure. He told me that my number plate did not conform to registration regulations and I was duly summoned to court where I was accused of putting illegal licence plates on my vehicle.

The local press and some of the nationals got wind of the case and so when I appeared at Romford Magistrates court the place was packed with sniffers and snorters – reporters.

I represented myself and pleaded not guilty. The first cop gave his statement, which I agreed with. Then the second one went into the dock and I asked him whether he'd measured both plates – because I knew he'd only measured the front one. When he admitted he'd only measured one, the old garden gate – the magistrate – said, 'So we are talking about a number plate, rather than number plates.'

Then I took the stand. I said, 'First and furthermost the charge sheet reads that I put these number plates on the car. I did not. They were put on the car by a garage mechanic working for Ford's at Dagenham' – this got a titter from the spectators. I went on. 'I'm afraid I can't tell you his name because we were never formally introduced' – more laughs. 'I have to tell you, sir, I was driving the car when the officer stopped me and I have been driving it for a considerable time. My name is Albert Simmonds, but my stage name is Jimmy Jones and 'U ME 1M' refers to one of my jokes. I travel the length and breadth of Britain and I have never ever been stopped before for having these plates.'

At this the copper gets up and he said: 'It may interest Mr Simmonds to know that I have never heard of Jimmy Jones.'

I said, 'Just a second your honour, he can't blame me for his misfortune.' And by this time the whole court was laughing. I'd made the copper look what he was – a twat. Even the beak was smiling. Then he turned to me and said, 'Have you anything else to say?'

'Yes,' I said. 'If having a personalised number plate is wrong I would like to inform the court that there is a car driving around London with the letters HRH on it as its plate.' Again the court laughed, but the magistrate said, 'We are not here to discuss HRH, we are here to talk about U ME 1M,' and he fined me £5.

I said, 'Can I have time to pay?... no, your honour, I'm only joking.' And I paid up a fiver, which as you will realise was a derisory sum back then.

By my reckoning that was game set and match to me. The copper obviously agreed because as I left the court he came up to me and snarled, 'You made me look an absolute cunt in there.'

I replied: 'Well, you cannot alter nature.'

He was furious. 'I'm telling you now I am going to fucking nick you whenever I fucking see you,' he growled, between gritted teeth. 'You are always going to be doing something wrong.'

'Hang on,' I said. 'That sounds like police harassment and a threat to me.' I turned to the gentleman standing beside me and said, 'Did you hear that?'

'Yes I did,' he said.

The cop turned on him and spat: 'It's got fuck all to do with you.'

The bloke said. 'I'm afraid you're wrong. It has a great deal to do with me, young man, because I am Inspector Payne from Upminster police station. I want you in my office in one hour's time.'

And that copper was moved down to traffic.

The Pope is over in Britain on a visit and he's late for a meeting with the Queen. So he asks his driver to put his foot down, but the man is adamant that he can't do more than 70mph. The Pope says, 'OK, I'll drive', and he gets in and puts his foot down: 70-80-90... and then this motorway cunt-stable pulls him up and when he sees who is in the driving seat he is straight on the radio. He says to his sergeant, 'Sarge, I don't like to do this but I've pulled someone up for speeding and he's important.'

The sergeant says, 'How important? Is it Prince Charles?' The cop says, 'No, he's more important than that.'

'Well who is it then?' asks the sergeant. The cop says, 'I don't know but the Pope is 'kin' driving him.'

CHAPTER EIGHTEEN
RACE: EQUAL OPPORTUNITIES OFFENDER

Irishman walked into a pub, a lump of dog shit in his hand. He said, 'I'm a lucky bastard, me, I nearly trod in that...'

Black fella walks into a watchmaker's, unzips his trousers and slaps his dick on the counter. The woman screams and says, 'You can't do that.' The fella says, 'This is a watchmaker's isn't it? Well, put a couple of hands on that.'

Any Irish in? You have to be careful. There's a lot of them about up here and if you upset them bastards they throw pins at you. And if they do fucking run 'cos they've got a hand grenade in their mouth...

I'm not having a go at Pakistanis. I think we've got one in the audience. No, he wouldn't have shut the shop this 'kin' early.

JIMMY JONES

I know a fella who once spent 30 years in darkest Africa looking for the lost Masazuki tribe. He eventually found them above a chip shop in Peckham.

An Irishman pulled over a lorry on the M1. He told the driver, 'I had to stop you, you're losing your load.' The driver said, 'I'm 'kin' gritting.'

Irish fella staying in a Blackpool guesthouse insisted on eating cold beans for breakfast every morning. After a week, the landlady had a knock on the door. It's the police telling her the Irish fella had killed himself. 'I can't understand that,' she said. 'He left here full of beans.'

I know a Scotsman who has crabs, he won't get rid of them 'cos he thinks they're money spiders.

I pulled a Scottish bird once, big fat girl she was, but she was keen. I got her back to the hotel and she stripped off. I thought this is not looking good 'cos it was a double bed and there was no room for me. I thought, I ain't getting on top, I'll burn me arse on the light bulb. So I turned the light off and that made it worse 'cos one of her tits fell out of the bed and smashed the ashtray. There was so much slapping about the bloke next door thought I was Morris dancing. I said, 'Could you fart and give us a clue?' and I found it.
I was banging away and she said, 'You've no got a very big organ.' I said, 'Well it's not used to playing in a cathedral.'

RACE: EQUAL OPPORTUNITIES OFFENDER

She said, 'Have you taken any precautions?' I said, 'Yeah, I've tied me foot to the bed post.'

I've got this Irish mate, a car mechanic, and I said to him, 'Hey Murphy, what do you think of the Renault 5?' He said, 'I don't think they're guilty.'

I've just come back from Dubai. The women over there walk around with 'kin' masks on. And there are flies. One particular fly is called the bobo fly and that is attracted to the arsehole of the camel. Well, I saw these two women and they were having a right ding-dong in Dubainese. So I asked a fella what was going on. He said they are arguing because one of the women told the other one that she had a bobo fly buzzing around her face. The other woman said, 'Are you saying I've got a face like a camel's arse?' Her friend replied, 'I ain't saying nothing but you ain't fooling that bobo fly.'

A Jewish boy comes home from school and tells his mother he's been given a part in the school play. 'Wonderful! What part is it?' The boy says, 'I play the part of the Jewish husband.' The mother scowls and says, 'You go back and tell the teacher you want a speaking part.'

I just got married again, I took the wife on honeymoon to Wales to Bangor.

Any Welsh people in? Yes? Fuck it. You get more than two of them in one place and the bastards form a choir.

I was down there in Wales doing a show and a fella said, 'Jonesy, have you ever been down a mine?' I said, 'No, round our way the coalmen deliver.' He said, 'Oh, you ought to try it before they shut them all down.' So I went to this pit. The lift down went so slow I thought it was broken. It was a mile and a quarter deep. Then they put me on a train to take me to the coal face to see the coal being dug. That was another hour and 25 minutes. No wonder we were fighting the 'kin' Germans, we were nicking their 'kin' coal...

I'VE ALWAYS TOLD jokes about everybody, every race and nationality. Whoever was in I'd have a gag for them. If there was an Italian in the audience I'd ask, why is Italy shaped like a boot? Cos you couldn't get all that shit in a sandal. If there was a bubble in, I'd say, in Greece how do you separate the men from the boys? With a crow bar! Why do Iraqi men grow moustaches? Because they want to look like their mothers... I had jokes about everybody.

By the late '80s there was a backlash against white comedians doing ethnic gags. It didn't make any difference to my TV appearances because I didn't have any, but various councils banned me from their venues on suspicion that I might be 'racist and sexist'. It was never the black people themselves who objected to me, though; it was always the white do-gooders who think I'm offending black people by doing accents.

The busy-bodies called me a racist but I don't hate anybody and I never have. And as for being a sexist, sure I tell gags about women, but I tell gags about men as well. Women can be far more hurtful than men. A woman can destroy a man with three words: 'Are you in?'

Years ago, one of the jokes the audiences always asked for was 'If You Like', about a cocky bloke who pulls a woman and gets her back to his place. He says things like, 'You can have a drink with me, if you like.' And she always answers, 'I will.' It ends up with him saying, 'You can sleep with me tonight, if you like' and her replying, 'I will!' Afterwards he says, 'In nine months time, you will have a baby, a baby boy, you can call him Peter, if you like.' The woman replies: 'In a fortnight's time you're going to break out in a rash. You can call it measles, if you like.' Now who is the loser there? The fella! He's the one who comes unstuck. With all jokes you have to ask, who is the victim here and what is the intention of the comedian.

Was I racist back in the day? No. Am I racist now? No. I don't hate anyone because of where they are from. You have to judge everyone as individuals. When I started doing the black voice back in the very early '70s, I was looking for a different way of telling jokes and I found that if I added a Jamaican accent the gag went better – I tried Welsh, Irish and Scottish too, but the Jamaican voice was the one that got the big laughs.

A London comedian called Peter Demmer was probably the biggest influence on me. I'd watch Demmer do his West Indian voice – which was completely different to mine – back at the Royal Standard, and I thought that's the way to do the gags.

Back then I was doing seven nights a week and Sunday lunch time. Sometimes I'd be on stage for 90 minutes, two hours, mostly one-liners, and the accent added variety and accents are funny. You see that on TV even now. Apu, the hard-working shopkeeper on *The Simpsons*, has a funny Indian accent, and the character is voiced by Hank Azaria, a New York comedian whose parents were Greek Jews. No one calls *The Simpsons* 'racist'. Even when Apu gets his citizenship and says, 'Yes! I am a citizen! Now, which way to the benefits office. I'm kidding, I'm kidding. I work, I work.'

The accent adds to the humour. You take my joke Pebble Glasses, among my audiences this was the most requested gag. Years ago when I put out a cassette of my Top 20 jokes, Pebble Glasses was Number One. It's all about a black lady called Lillibell who wants a divorce from her husband because of his unreasonable behaviour. She goes to court and tells the judge all about how her husband came home to find her at home with her daughter from a previous marriage and her friend with the pebble glasses. The husband sticks Lillibell's head up the chimney and gives her a right large portion from behind. The judge says, 'This man is an exhibitionist.' He then sticks the daughter's head in the banisters and pushes a large portion of helmet right up her harry-hole without lubrication. The judge says, 'This man is a tear-arse.' Then finally he takes her friend with the pebble glasses and ties each foot to opposite ends of the sofa and giving her the largest portion of helmet I ever saw a woman take. Finally he takes those pebble glasses, sticks them on the end of his knob and says, 'Now you take a good look around boy, make sure you ain't missed anybody.'

Now if you try and analyse that joke it isn't particularly funny in itself. The impact is all in the telling. It's the accent that makes it work. Take the accent away and you kill the gag. Black people in the audience always loved it. No black celebrity I've ever worked to has ever complained about my West Indian voice. Eddy Grant is a fan. John Conteh is a fan, Frank Bruno, Clem Curtis...

Back in 1972, I was working for a fella called Scott Walker who virtually booked the whole of the Midlands. He put me in Barbarella's, a nightclub in the centre of Birmingham where Duran Duran would start out playing a few years after. I should point out that Barbarella's was owned by the Fewtrell brother Chris and Eddie who were, if you like, the Krays of Birmingham. I was appearing there as the compère and top of the bill were the legendary American doo-wop group The Drifters. I had to think of a way of introducing these fellas in a funny way, so on the first night I said, 'Ladies and Gentlemen, here's a bunch of coloured fellas who appeared on *Opportunity Knocks* and had 14 nights' work cancelled, please put your hands together for The Drifters.' Well they weren't standing for that. They chased me all over the stage! They were laughing but they wanted to teach me a lesson, and so they tied me up and they left me sitting in the dressing room until 2am. Drifters singer Johnny Moore was killing himself laughing.

Johnny loved my statue gag in particular. It's about the West Indian fella who wins the pools, buys a big mansion and tells the designer he wants a statue in each room. He comes back and finds all these lovely Michelangelo statues everywhere. He says, 'No you silly bastard, I didn't mean a statue, I meant 'Is-dat-you?' (Mimes answering a telephone) Another accent joke that got big laughs at the time. I did that one on *The Comedians*.

I was doing all my West Indian accents and jokes with The Drifters and they seemed to love it all. They finished up asking for me to be the compère for all of their shows except for clubs where a front man had already been booked. We did two weeks at Barbarella's, we did the Cedar Club, Abigail's and the King's too – all of them in Birmingham. We did a lot of work together and became firm friends.

I worked with them again sometime after that at Jollee's in Stoke, and when I was doing my show at the Circus Tavern they were quite regular visitors. If The Drifters weren't offended by me, a band of black performers who had grown up in the USA when society was really segregated, why should I worry about what some soppy councillor or a snooty BBC producer thinks?

I've only ever had complaints from white people, the kind of people who are always looking to be offended on someone else's behalf.

Another fella who seemed to enjoy my act was Cass Pennant, the West Ham football hooligan turned writer. That bastard Bushell made me get up and do some gags at his book launch.

Cass was there. Now, Cass is about six foot four and as black as Newgate's knocker, and a Cockney boy. I kept one eye on him and when he started laughing I knew I'd be all right.

What was true of Pebble Glasses was true of the other gags I did. Like Trobbin' Pain, about the fella who has a ten-inch chopper growing out of his forehead. Or the little kid who kills a butterfly. His father is horrified and says because of that you'll have no butter for a week. Then the boy kills a honey bee and the dad says because of that you'll have no honey for a week. When they get home the kid sees his mum kill a big cockroach, then looks at his dad and says, 'Are you going to tell her or am I?'

The West Indian accent is wonderful. Listen to Patrick Truman on *EastEnders*, what a rich voice that is. It sounds funny even when he isn't saying anything funny. It's the cadence. I do the black accent much less now because less black people talk like that now. I still do the Pakistani voice though, and that's funny too.

I'll do a gag like, what does the average Pakistani weigh? Sweets. That isn't racist. That's observation. Because most of the Asian people most of us come into contact with are likely to be shopkeepers working bloody long hours or working in a restaurant.

I've had two TV documentaries made about me that were never shown – one was stopped by Michael Grade himself when he was running Channel 4. They said it was because I was too blue, but that's ridiculous, how can I be too blue when Billy Connolly's on there effing and blinding? I'm convinced I was banned from TV purely because of the false accusations that I'm a racialist. But what can you do? Everyone who knows me knows the truth.

I do eff and blind now on stage, because the days of Kinnell are gone and in a way it's a shame. There was more finesse then. But you have to move with the times.

I never set out to be an outrageous comic. I always wanted to be naughty. My all-time favourite gag is about the Heinz Beans addict and his wind problem. When I have caused offence, it's usually been by accident. The classic occasion was when I was appearing at the Wellington Pier in Great Yarmouth; and an old girl walked out of the show complaining, 'It's bloody disgusting in there.' Marion was outside on the stall and she said, 'You knew what you were in for at a Jimmy Jones show.' The old lady replied, 'That's just it, I thought I was going to see *Jack* Jones.'

The wind had blown the 'Jimmy' off the billing at the front of the pier – all you could see was Jones. Poor cow.

Another time, in Bournemouth, Marion heard these two old dears talking outside the Tregonwell Hall when I was on there. Lovely old ladies, they were. They looked like they could have just come from the audience of *Stars On Sunday*.

'Shall we go in and see him?' asked one. 'No,' said the other, 'he'll be too fucking filthy for us.'

*   *   *   *

I was with Clem Curtis the first time I encountered real blatant racism. He'd invited me down to the Q Club, a black nightclub in Bayswater to watch him perform with The

Foundations. I'd taken a party down from my pub: my wife Grace, my girlfriend Marion, my daughter Helen, my son Simmo and the DJ Tony 'Shades' Valance. We were the only white people in there. Everyone else was black. It was baking hot in this club and after a while Marion went outside to have a fag and put her cardigan in the car. But then the doorman wouldn't let her back in. He called her a 'honky' and everything. After a while I started to worry and went looking for her. I found her sitting in the car and she explained what had happened. When I went to go back in and they wouldn't let me in either. I explained that I was with Clem Curtis and that my wife and kids were in there, and this doorman said, 'Well go in, get your crowd and fuck off. This is a black club. It's for Rastafarians. It's not for you.' Charming.

CHAPTER NINETEEN

IN THE COURT OF
THE SUN KING

BACK IN 1988, Garry Bushell got me a nice little job for the editor of *The Sun*, Kelvin MacKenzie. It was for Kelvin's wife Jackie's 40th birthday at the Savoy in London. The deal was my fee would go to charity. I asked for £600 for Great Ormond Street Hospital and Kelvin gave £800 instead. It wasn't quite as simple as it seemed, though.

I'd thought I was performing at a private party for 40 people. It was actually 14 people, including Kelvin's mum and his 12-year-old son, and just before I went on Kelvin took me to one side, and said ''Ere Jones, no sex jokes, all right?' No sex jokes! That was half the act gone. I made a surprise entrance, Jackie was thrilled, and I thought the easiest way to do it was to go round all 14 people and ask them each to pick a subject for a joke. Of course when I got to the kid, he gave a big grin and said, 'SEX!'

I worked for Kelvin again years later when he was running a cable channel called Live TV, which was full of trampolining dwarves, Norwegian weathergirls and other daft things. He called up and asked if I'd come in and do some gags. But – there's always a but! – they had no budget and would I do it for nothing... typical television. I agreed but then I had quite a few rows with the producers because they expected me to pay my own car-parking fees while I was performing. Bad enough that they wanted me to do my act for nothing, but the tight bastards wanted me to be out of pocket too. I kicked up a stink and as far as I know I was the only act that made them pay for car parking.

Most of the private shows I've done have been for villains. I've done shows for gangsters in Blackpool, Stockport, Middlesbrough, Newcastle and even Spain. The most recent one was for a villain who has to live on a boat that is moored off of North Africa so he can't be extradited back home to face trial. None of them have expected me to do it for nothing, though. All those crooks and the only one who tried to rob me was Kelvin!

A few years after my private gig for Mr MacKenzie, I invited a bunch of friendly *Sun* journalists along to the Tandoori Parlour, in Thundersley, Essex. There were Garry Bushell, Garry Johnson, Antonella Lazzeri and a couple of others. This was a great place, an Indian restaurant run by a couple of Stepney-born Bengalis, which put on comedians while people were eating. Halfway through the act I mentioned that my dog had gone missing and asked the waiter if I could look in his kitchen. Some woman in the audience went potty. Then to make it worse, one of the two Garrys put

Antonella up to request my pebble glasses gag. The same woman walked out, and the audiences booed her. The staff loved it. They even gave me a doggy bag. My dog wasn't in it.

I like Indian food, especially the really hot ones that they keep the toilet rolls in the fridge for. You ever had that the morning after a vindaloo where your arsehole is so sore it looks like the flag of Japan? You sit on the pan and your arse dives down and drinks the water. No wonder Ghandi wore a nappy. Those poor Indians only ever see us when we're pissed. They get all these mouthy blokes going in, 'Come on Ramsammy, get us a pint.' That's when they get their own back, they go back in the kitchen and say, 'This one has got to suffer, give him the burning bum.'

CHAPTER TWENTY

A CELEBRITY AUDIENCE WITH JIMMY JONES

THE SUN ALWAYS used to campaign for more Jimmy Jones on TV. Garry Bushell said they should give me *An Audience With*. But the more the paper said it, the more television people dug their heels in against me. The *Audience With* suggestion was a great idea but it was never going to happen. So I thought, why not do my own? Neil Warnock thought this was a terrific thing to set up and we got a video company who were keen to film it. But where should it be done? The early pubs I'd worked were either closed or too small or grotty; the Circus Tavern wasn't right either because it was too big to be intimate. It needed to be a TV studio or a theatre. Then it occurred to me. Royal Windsor had always been a centre of English cultural and intellectual debate. So why shouldn't the next stage in Windsor's proud history be *A Celebrity Audience With Jimmy Jones*?

We hired the Theatre Royal, just around the corner from Windsor Castle, and invited a load of my friends from showbiz and rock'n'roll. To my amazement on the day, when we got there for the run through, there was a small group protesting outside the theatre, saying 'We don't want Jimmy Jones in our town'. It's a shame there weren't a few more of them because that would have got us in the papers. The theatre staff were all pretty prudish about it too – the usherettes all had their noses in the air. In-house director Mark Piper, who's married to Sue Holderness who plays Marlene in *Only Fools & Horses*, didn't seem especially thrilled. But a lot of people were because on the night it was sold out.

The public had come from miles around, and the celebs turned out in force. There was Rick Parfitt from Status Quo, Martine McCutcheon and Dean Gaffney from *EastEnders*, Jess Conrad, Helen Keating from *London's Burning*, and of course Nicko McBrain from Iron Maiden. We even invited Garry Bushell along and stuck him in the royal box so I could open the show by saying, 'Oi, I've heard it's *Bushell on the Box* but you're in the wrong 'kin' box, son. You'll have to move...' Then I pretended to find out that Her Majesty wasn't coming in person, and said: 'Well if she ain't coming, fuck her.'

I had to explain to those who hadn't seen me for a while that my old catchphrase Kinnell was no more. Kinnell had turned to fuck. Literally. I had to move with the times and these days you had to say the word fuck or you wouldn't get an 18 certificate on your videos or DVDs. But, as I explained, there are a lot worse words on TV. You hear the word 'kill' every day on TV, don't you? I said, you ask any of these ladies down here at the front, isn't 'kill' a horrible word? What would you rather be, killed or fucked?

I also had to explain that I was still banned from TV, and the fuckers wouldn't let me on *Rosie & Jim*, which I found disappointing.

Have you ever seen *Rosie & Jim*? What an ugly pair of bastards…

There were a lot of stars in, as I said, and to be honest I was bricking it a bit – I'd been on the khazi the best part of the afternoon. It's a great tribute when other performers turn out for you. One of the guests I was most pleased to see was a young girl I'd first met way back in the early '70s when she was a struggling actress. I'd gone for a meal at Yips, a big Chinese restaurant in Tooting, South London and there was a young girl outside whose face I recognised from the TV. It was Pauline Quirke, who was then a teenager. She was in a couple of TV shows, she was appearing as a school kid in one of the programmes, so I invited her and her friend to come in and join us. She said, 'I can't come in, Mr Jones, we ain't got no money.'

'You don't need money,' I said. 'I'll buy the meal. You look like you could do with fattening up.'

So they came and ate with us and Pauline had a very healthy appetite as it happens, and so did her friend. And she went on to be a big TV star, with her hit sitcom *Birds of a Feather* and shows like *Maisie Raine* where she played a cop, and now she is going into *Emmerdale*. So good luck to her.

I was very pleased that Pauline came to my Audience With and even more pleased when she reminded me of that day back when she was a kid. If you watch the tape back, one of the things she says to me is, 'I still owe you a meal.' Now isn't that nice? All those years later and she still remembered. Now that's what I thought most of the people in the entertainment business would be like. And some of them were. We are still good friends. We don't live in each other's pockets, but if she picked up the phone and asked me for a favour she'd get it, and vice versa.

*   *   *   *

I did another DVD in 2008, *The Guv'nor's Last Stand*, filmed at the Circus Tavern, which had some very nice tributes from Frank Carson, Chubby, Jim Bowen, Jim Davidson and other great friends I've made over the years. It was another full house. You have to go out to have a laugh now – there's nothing funny on TV.

CHAPTER TWENTY-ONE

IF I WERE THE MARION KIND

The doctor asked, 'Do you ever talk to your wife when you're having intercourse?'

I said, 'It depends if there's a 'kin' phone handy.'

MY DIVORCE COST me £1 million. I knew the day was going to go badly. My hearing was in Court 13 at the Old Bailey with the same woman judge who dealt with Jim Davidson when his marriage to Tracy Hilton went tits-up in 2000. What chance did I have?

Two years later it was my turn to be hung out to dry. Robin Williams said that divorce came from the Latin word meaning to rip out a man's genitals through his wallet. He's not wrong.

It turns out that alimony turned out to be short for all the money...

But that's the price you pay for being happy.

I never wanted a divorce and I never ever wanted to hurt Gracie. I always said to my kids, I did not divorce your mother, your mother divorced me. My family has always been the most important thing in my life and I really believed in keeping the family together – even if it meant I didn't really see the kids growing up because I was running around like a blue-arsed fly to keep food on the table.

I never meant to fall in love with Marion, and although I did, I never ever forsook my wife and kids. If Grace hadn't divorced me, I would probably still be leading a double life, running two homes and living with two women.

The divorce came out of the blue. After 45 years of marriage I really wasn't expecting it. Especially as Grace had known about me and Marion for 34 years. She admitted that at the divorce hearing. It was an unspoken thing. We didn't flaunt it in her face and most of the time she just accepted it, although there were a couple of times when she decided to try and catch us out. The most spectacular occasion was while I was down working at King's in Eastbourne.

Now, I am a firm believer in clairvoyants. I used to go and see one called Ruby regularly in Tottenham. Once when I was down in Eastbourne I got a call at the hotel from Barbara Thorpe, an actress friend who'd just been for a sitting with Ruby. Ruby had told her to pass on the message that I was going to get a surprise visit from my wife. She said I had to get Marion out of the hotel, and put her on the train to Waterloo where Barbara very kindly agreed to meet her and help her get home. Well, I did as she said; I dropped Marion off at the station, got back to the hotel and I hadn't been there ten minutes when there was a bang on the door and there was

Grace with my eldest son. He said, 'Dad, there was no way I could warn you.' She hadn't caught me out, though, so there was no harm done, but how do you explain that? Even Derren Brown couldn't find a hole in that.

Most of the time Grace accepted the situation, because it suited her too. Marion and I went on holiday together for 15 years and nothing was ever said. She came on holiday with me and Grace, we went out as a threesome. Freddie Starr used to say, 'Fuck me Jonesy, I don't know how you get away with it 'cos I get caught every time.'

I got away with it because it suited everybody. Grace turned a blind eye to what was going on because Marion was doing something that she did not want to do, as explained earlier in this book.

The other reason it suited her that I had Marion to go places with was Grace hated the business. She loved the rewards of my job but she hated showbusiness and everything to do with it.

I met Marion, as I've said elsewhere, when she was 18 and an absolute stunner, and we've been together for 40 years – since 1966 to the present day. She's 61 now, but you'd think she was 55. She's still a looker.

Marion became part of the family. I initially got her into my house by making her pretend to be my brother-in-law's girlfriend. Marion and Grace became friends; she helped bring up some of the kids. When I got caught misbehaving with another other woman, Grace actually turned to Marion and her exact words were, 'Look what that dirty bastard's done to us!'

Grace forgave me, Marion didn't. She made me suffer for a month over that. I never did it again.

Everything changed the moment my mother-in-law died. On the Sunday straight after that Grace said, 'I want you out of my house.' Not our house. She said, 'I don't like your business and I don't like the people you mix with.'

So I moved out, and moved in with Marion.

I was never entirely sure what made Grace go for a divorce. I'm fairly certain that someone in the family persuaded her to do it, and it was ever so well planned. On the day the divorce papers were served, the locks on my two villas in Menorca were also changed and it was the same with the place in Florida. Someone helped with the planning and execution of that, and it was done with maximum effect to hurt me hard.

But I never wanted to hurt anybody. I did what I did to keep my family together and to keep sane, but of course Marion became more like a wife to me and I suppose that it was inevitable that when I was finally free she would become my wife for real.

After my divorce, Marion and I went to make our wills. The solicitor asked, 'Are you going to marry her, because if you don't she will have to pay 40 per cent tax on everything you leave her.'

'We'd better get married, then,' I said.

The solicitor laughed. 'That's the most romantic proposal I've ever heard,' he said.

And that was it. We got married in 2005 at Langton House, a beautiful Georgian listed building in Hornchurch, Essex. We're very happy with our life together and I hope that if Grace is reading this book that she is very happy with her life as well.

CHAPTER TWENTY-TWO

THE WORST NEWS IN THE WORLD

A WHILE AGO I received the worst news a parent could ever hear. My eldest daughter Helen had terminal cancer and unfortunately we lost her before this book was published. No father wants to bury his own child and it breaks my heart just thinking about it. Over her last months, I would frequently wake up in the middle of the night and have to get up because I couldn't get back to sleep for thinking about her. It was heartbreaking watching her deteriorate.

Please God, she is up above looking down on us, reunited with the family I've lost, my brothers and sisters and my mum and dad. Because all of us believe that there is life after death.

Helen had cancer of the bowel to start with and then it moved to her lungs. She wasn't afraid of dying, her only fear was for her son who is ten – and that's young to lose your mother, but he'll have a lot of family around him. The boy will be looked after well.

I was always close to Helen. She was the first one of my

family ever to keep a diary on my success and a scrap book for my press cuttings. She was always very proud of her dad – and I've always been proud of her, and the rest of my children.

Even in her final months, Helen was still laughing a lot; she had a wonderful sense of humour. Other cancer sufferers used to ask to book their chemo when she was there with her sister Dolly because the two of them laughed so much. And when I was with them they laughed even more because they were taking the piss out of me. Everyone loved Helen. She used to work at Makro and the staff still had collections for her every month until she passed because she was so popular.

Helen believed in clairvoyants, as I do, and she was always threatening to come back and take the piss out of me some more from the other side. When the TV psychic Sally Morgan appeared at the Cliff's Pavilion in Southend-on-Sea earlier this year, Dolly took Helen along to see her. She was in her wheelchair but the soppy bastards put them up in the gallery. Dolly said, 'Are you having a laugh? She's in a wheelchair,' so the theatre staff took them to the wheelchair access area. It was packed by this time and everyone had to stand up to let us get past. Then, after disturbing everyone opening her sweets, Helen's leg started shaking. She turned to Dolly and said, 'I need to go,' and then she stood up and walked to the loo. Everyone was looking at them, the punters, the theatre staff, all of them thinking, She ain't really a wheelchair case, she's using that chair to get down the front.

She was planning her own funeral months in advance. She

told me that she wanted me and her four brothers to carry her, plus her two brothers-in-law, and then she said, 'And what about him and him...' I said, 'What do you think you'll be coming home in – a 12-foot coffin?'

We had to laugh our way through it, it's the English way.

Helen also insisted on knowing how I would like to go. Without hesitation I replied, 'Like my granddad.'

'How did he pass?' she asked?

I told her that he had just sat in a chair, his head dropped back, his mouth fell open and he went. It was a beautiful death.

Mind you, it frightened the life out of the dentist.

*   *   *

I'm proud of all my family. Paul is 52 now and has his own fencing company. Helen is 51, she was a publican – she started early in my pub. Steven is 50 and a jack-of-all-trades. Graham, 49, has a groundwork company, Annette, 45, who I call Dolly describes herself as a 'go-fer' and my youngest, Peter, 43, has dry-cleaning shops. The only one of my children who has caused me grief is my son Steven, who is known by everyone as Simmo. He's the wayward son. He started going off the rails at an early age. Even as a kid he was always out with me in the car because if I left him behind he'd give his mother stick. We took him to a Harley Street psychiatrist and after a consultation the gentleman said, 'There is nothing wrong with your son, he has one of the cutest minds I've ever encountered and he is a pleasure to talk to. All he wants to be in life is his father, he wants to be Jimmy Jones.'

Well, Simmo did take after his father in one respect – he was murder when it came to women. At one stage when I was down in Bournemouth he was knocking off a singer and her sister. Like father, like son. It's hard for a bloke to resist sex when you're offered it on a plate. I've always said that a standing prick has no conscience.

To keep him out of trouble I got him to work for me. He was my roadie and my driver. At the time I was working for all Bob Wheatley's venues – he had one in Leicester and Westcombe as well as the Tavern. On a Sunday I was still working at King's with strippers and comedians like Harry Scott.

Truth be told, Simmo could have followed me into the business. He has a very good voice and he is much wittier than I am. But he dries up at the thought of doing it in public. And, besides, Simmo has always been in to all sorts of skulduggery. Where I helped myself to anything I could get hold of in the docks he helped himself to anything that wasn't nailed down. Give him enough rope and he'd have tied a cashier up with it. He stole from me, he stole from friends, he stole from Neil Warnock and I'll admit now that I was in the wrong because I encouraged people not to prosecute him and have him punished for what he was doing. I turned on the charm and replaced what was missing and tried to sweep it under the carpet.

He started selling drugs at one stage and dropping the name of a major villain in Essex as back-up. When the gentleman in question got wind of it he phoned me up. 'If Simmo does it again I'm going to have to charge him for it,' he said. 'If he's using my name it comes with a price.'

THE WORST NEWS IN THE WORLD

The longer it went on unchecked the worse Simmo got. In the end he went to prison three times. The sentences were always short term – six months here, nine months there. He was supposed to do seven years on one occasion but that was shortened because he agreed to go into rehab.

My mate Mickey is in prison for something he didn't do – he didn't run fast enough. He used to say, 'Jim, crime doesn't pay – but the hours are good.'

Some arsehole broke into my house the other day. He didn't take jewellery, he didn't take money and he didn't take the TV. All he took was the remote control. And now the rotten bastard drives past every night and changes the channel.

EPILOGUE

'OLD ON, I'M COMING

WELL, THAT WAS my story, warts and all. I hope you enjoyed it and that you laughed enough to want to come and see one of my shows because I'm due to retire but I never will. I tell people I'm semi-retired. But when you've been a performer all your life you never want to stop. A charity gig will come in, or a golf day. Now there's a tour to promote this book, and the DVD that goes with it. There's always a reason not to stop.

The laughs never seem to stop either. I was driving home from a gig just a couple of weeks ago and I was breaking my neck for a Jimmy Riddle. So I pulled up on the motorway and had a wee under a bridge. There was a phone right by me which rang as I was finishing. It was a copper. He said to me, 'You realise, sir, that you are being watched on camera?' I replied, 'Haven't I got a beauty?' And then I put the phone down and drove off.

Another time recently I had a puncture on the A2, pulled

over and realised I had no jack in the car. So I called out the AA. A bloke came, he jacked up the car, took out the spare and then realised that was punctured too. He said he'd take it away and repair it but he needed a £50 deposit on the jack. When I asked why, he said 'In case you've gone when I come back.' I said 'Where the kinnell am I going to go on three wheels?' But he was serious and I had to give him a bulls-eye before he'd go and fix the tyre.

I'm still in touch with all the old comedians. I worry about dear old Frank Carson. I was at a dinner with him just a few weeks ago and he started to tell the same gag for the third time. I said, 'Frank, you've already told this one twice.' He said, 'I'm telling it again just to make sure you're listening.'

Jim Bowen has pretty much given up comedy. All he does now is cruises. He drives down to Southampton, gets on a boat for two weeks, does one show on the way out and another on the way back. But he doesn't tell any jokes at all, he just sits there and talks about *Bullseye*.

It's a tough time to be a comic over the age of 50. Comedy has got very snooty again and, unless you're young and fashionable with a degree in bollockology, television bosses don't want to know. I watch stuff on TV that is supposed to be funny and I just don't get it. I'm not slagging off the performers – good luck to them. But now a comedian is considered a hit if he gets 3 million viewers. *The Comedians* used to get 15 million viewers every week.

TV has turned its back on humour that everyday people like and I think that's a shame. And the language! As you'll now know I had murders with television bosses back when the rudest thing I ever said was 'Kinnell'. George Carlin the great American comedian used to have a routine called the seven words you can never say on TV. Those words were shit, piss, fuck, cunt, cocksucker, motherfucker and tits. Now you hear most of those words every night on TV, three of them before the watershed. What used to be banned now seems to be compulsory.

Younger comics tease me about my age now. Mickey Pugh says I'm so old my blood type is discontinued. Dave Lee reckons that when I go into a cafe and order a three-minute egg they make me pay upfront. And I know that I am getting on because when I walk past an antique shop I remember owning half the furniture in there. But the important thing is I don't feel old. As far as I'm concerned 'old' is 15 years from now.

I may not be as fit as I was and it might take a little longer for little Jim to rise to the occasion, but I've still got my wits about me. It's true that my hearing has got worse over the years. It hasn't stopped me working, though, and I hope it never will. I'd like to go out like Tommy Cooper, falling over on stage with the laughter still echoing round my earholes. That's the way a comic goes. Not with a whimper but with a standing ovation.

This pensioner pulled a barmaid the other night, a real cracker she was. She took him back to her place and said, 'What do you like in bed?' He said, 'Guard rails.'
A fella I know in Eastbourne lost his virginity at 93. He

wanted to tell his mates about it but they were all dead. Mind you, everyone down there is old. In Eastbourne they've got a branch of Next and it's a funeral parlour.

You take your life in your hands having sex at that age. One minute you're saying 'Oh God, oh God', the next it's, 'Hello, God!'

Frank Carson is getting on now. He's so old he needs Viagra just to raise his hand.

THE FULL MONTY
VIDEOS AND DVDS

1982 *Live At Kings*

1987 *Newmarket Classic*

1989 *As It Happened – An Audience with The Guv'nor*

1989 *The Best Of Jimmy Jones*

1990 *A Cultural Night Out*

1991 *Twice As Outrageous*

1992 *Harder and Faster*

1994 *Barefaced Cheek*

1995 *Cock-ups and Boobs*

1997 *Tickle My Tackle*

1999 *As Good As Gold*

2002 *A Celebrity Audience With Jimmy Jones*

2008 *The Guv'nor's Last Stand*